The F vigator

Thomas Krause

First edition

August 2010

Published by BG Consulting Group Ltd. 2010

BG Consulting Group Ltd.
7 Harp Lane
London
EC3R 6DP
United Kingdom
www.bgconsulting.com

About the Author

Thomas Christian Krause

Thomas is an experienced professional in the area of capital markets and financial derivatives. He joined BG Consulting Group, a London based provider of high quality, tailored and practical training solutions to the financial service sector, in 2007. Since then, he has trained traders, middle-office, back-office and IT staff from leading investment banks, asset management companies and other financial institutions in Europe and Asia.

He began his career in finance in 1998 in one of the biggest German mortgage banks. As a member of the ALM Team, he managed the bank's interest rate risk in all major currencies for more than six years and specialised in trading interest rate derivatives. In 2000, he started to read economics and business management alongside work and graduated four years later with a diploma in banking and management from the University of Applied Sciences Kaiserslautern.

In late 2005, Thomas was appointed to set up the Derivative Strategies and Trading Team in one of the largest Asset Management companies in Europe. In the process, he introduced several derivative instruments to the company, implemented modern portfolio management concepts and successful overlay trading for both fixed income and equity funds.

After incidentally meeting one of his current colleagues and being taken in by his stories of the glamorous life as a trainer, he joined BG Consulting in March 2007 and specialises in training interest rate, equity and FX derivatives.

To Marina and “the guys” in Mexico City.

Table of Content

1

Derivatives Fundamentals

Derivatives are probably the most controversially discussed financial instruments – not just since the excessive use of complex structured derivatives was identified as one of the main origins of the global financial crisis which loomed in summer 2007.

In 2003, Alan Greenspan postulated that "derivatives have been an extraordinarily useful vehicle to transfer risk from those who shouldn't be taking it to those who are willing to and are capable of doing so" and that it therefore is a mistake to deeply regulate these contracts. However, at the same time, Warren Buffet observed that derivatives were "financial weapons of mass destruction, carrying dangers that, while now latent, are potentially lethal."

So whose standpoint is right? As so often in life, the truth probably lies somewhere in the middle. Managing financial risks will certainly be a lot more difficult without the use of derivatives; hedging costs will potentially increase while hedging accuracy will diminish. In fact, the risk transfer functionality of derivatives is something no financial expert will ever criticise. The problem is that derivatives are not only used to lower risk but also to increase it. And it was this accumulation of risks or – in financial terms – leverage that lead to the spectacular blowouts which brought the financial system to the edge of extinction and fuelled the already bad reputation of derivatives in public. This book does not aim to be a defence paper for derivatives but, hopefully, this chapter will point out that derivatives are very important for the efficiency of modern financial markets and if used responsibly, are not riskier than a direct position in the underlying itself.

1.1 What is a derivative?

Before joining the discussion, you might want to know exactly what a derivative is. Here follows a generic definition: a derivative is a financial instrument that is derived from an underlying asset (for example a bond, a stock, a currency, a commodity, etc.). Depending on the way the contract is designed, derivatives can be categorised into four main classes: forwards, futures, swaps and options. As this book is about forwards and futures, so we will concentrate on these contracts alone.

1.1.1 Forwards

Forwards are tradable on many different underlyings (currencies, interest rates, shares, commodities) and depending on the type of underlying, the mechanics of forwards differ marginally. It is important to understand these underlying specific features in order to apply them correctly but at this point, let us have a look at the general principles that are applicable for every forward contract. A forward is:

- A contract to buy or sell another financial instrument (the underlying) at a future date with price, quantity, etc. specified today
- A financial instrument whose value depends on the value of the underlying at a future date
- Settled in the future[1]

---

[1] The term settlement describes the completion of liabilities resulting from a financial transaction (for example, cash for security). Depending on the time lag between conclusion of the deal and the settlement, market practitioners distinguish between spot and future settlement. The spot market is defined as a market in which financial assets are sold for cash

These bullet points can be clarified best using a concrete example. Let us assume that Air France has just ordered five new Boeing 777 planes which will be delivered in one year from now. Apart from the initial deposit, the payment – 1 billion US dollars ($) – will be made upon delivery and the amount is denominated in $. As Air France accounts in euros (€), the commitment to the $ payment results in a foreign exchange risk. The current €/$ exchange rate is 1.46 (quoted in $ per €) so that the contract value in € currently is 684,931,506.85.

The problem: the $ amount is due in a year's time and exchange rates can be very volatile (from year end 2006 to year end of 2007, the currency pair moved from 1.3201 to 1.4592 with highs at 1.2893 and lows at 1.4872). As the airline has to buy $ to pay for the planes, there is the risk of an appreciation of the $ – which in this currency pair will be reflected in a falling number, as a $ appreciation means that one gets less $ for every € sold.

To eliminate the FX risk, the airline decides to enter into an FX forward transaction. Within this contract, the airline agrees today to buy $ 1 billion from the counterparty for a fixed amount of €. The € amount is set at 684,697,021.57, which implies an exchange rate (also referred to as the price) of:

$$\frac{1{,}000{,}000{,}000}{684{,}697{,}021.57} = 1.4605$$ [2]

The settlement of this contract will take place in the future – accordingly, the first and third bullet points are reflected in this explanation.

---

and delivered immediately. However, immediate delivery in financial markets should not be taken literally: in most spot markets, it is convention to settle the trade two or even three bank days after the trade has been agreed. If the settlement is agreed to take place later than these two or three days, this is referred to as future settlement.

[2] Why the forward exchange rate differs from the spot exchange rate and how the forward price is calculated will be discussed in detail in Chapter 2.

But why does the value of the transaction depend on the value of the underlying at a future time?

So far, we have looked at derivatives from a hedging perspective – the airline entered into the agreement in order to eliminate an FX risk. Let us now assume that the user of the derivative is not a hedger but a trader and he believes that the $ is going to appreciate and therefore enters into the forward transaction as described above. The future settlement of the FX forward can be illustrated as follows:

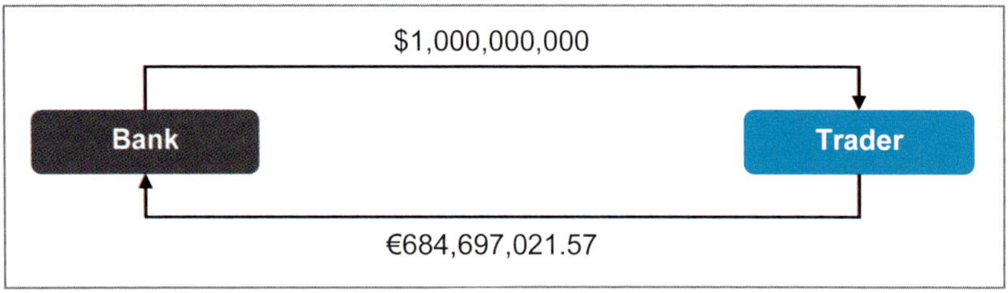

A year later, the €/$ exchange rate trades at 1.35 – so the $ has appreciated. As the trader neither has an interest to receive the $ nor has the € amount that is required for the settlement of the FX forward, he sells the $ at the spot market and receives €740,740,740.74.

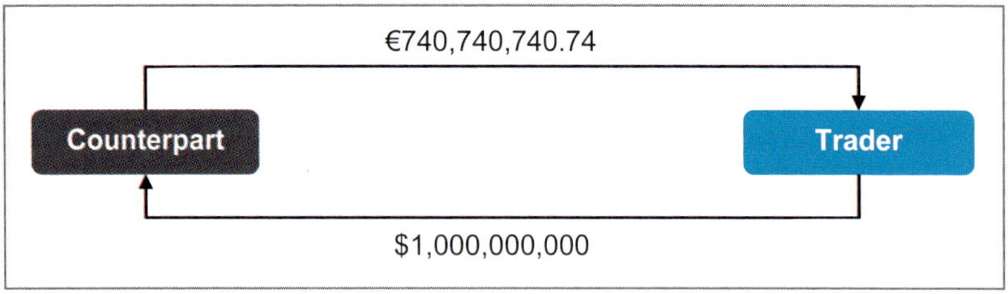

Within the forward contract, the trader agreed to buy $ at a price agreed today. As the $ appreciated during the forward period, this agreement turned out to be advantageous, as the trader could sell the $ for a higher € amount than initially paid. The trader is left with a profit of:

$$740{,}740{,}740.74 - 684{,}697{,}021.57 = €56{,}043{,}719.17$$

The amount of the profit clearly depends on the spot exchange rate for €/$ at the settlement date, so it is correct to say that a forward is a contract whose value depends on the value of the underlying at a future time – which was stated in the second bullet point of our initial definition.

1.1.2 Futures

Derivatives are traded in two different ways: Over The Counter (OTC) or through a formal exchange.

Forwards are OTC instruments: they are bilaterally agreed between the two counterparties who can "freely" decide the terms of the deal. However, a great number of derivative contracts are traded through formal exchanges like NYSE Euronext, EUREX or CME.

Futures rank among these exchange-traded derivatives. They are exchange-traded, legally binding agreements between two parties (the buyer and the seller) to deal in a specified underlying at a specific future date at a price agreed at the time of dealing. In other words, futures are exchange-traded forward contracts.

The benefit of futures in comparison to forwards lies in the usually narrower bid/offer spread and in the fact that there is a central observable market price, whereas OTC instruments often require proprietary models to value them. However, exchange trading requires contract standardisation and that is why the choice and therefore the flexibility in using futures contracts are limited.

Swaps

Financial swaps are OTC traded agreements between two counterparties to exchange two streams of cash flows. These cash flows are not predetermined at the moment of trading but depend on future developments of the underlying.

The most important swap type is the interest rate swap: an agreement to exchange a fixed rate of interest for a floating rate of interest. As shown in the following example, these contracts are often used to manage interest rate risks.

Example

A company borrowed $10 million for five years from a bank. As it is the case for most corporate loans, the agreement provides for a floating interest rate payment – the coupon formula is 6M $ LIBOR + 1.80%. The amount of interest is therefore not fixed but depends on future developments of short-term $ interest rates.

To increase cash flow planning reliability, the corporate treasurer enters into an interest rate swap where the company pays the fixed rate and receives 6M LIBOR for the next five years. Assuming a fixed rate of 3.75% is currently available, the floating rate loan has synthetically been transformed into a fixed rate loan with a coupon of 5.55% (3.75% + 1.80%):

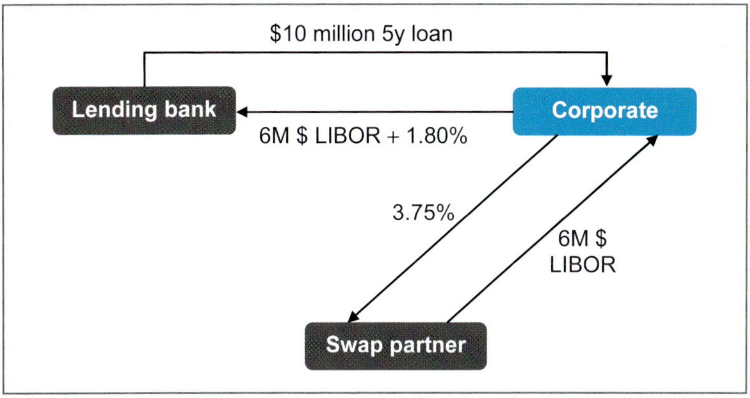

Please note that due to the different payment frequencies of the fixed rate and the floating rate (annually vs. semi-annually) this simple calculation of the fixed funding costs is not 100% accurate but provides a good gauge.

Options

The types of derivatives we have seen so far all have one common feature: their risk profile is symmetric.

Let us go back to forwards: a trader expects the share price of Ford Motor Co. to rise from its current level of $8.40 to above $10 within a year. The 1y forward price is $8.50 and the trader buys 1 million shares on a 1y forward basis. If in a year's time, the share price is above $8.50, the trader makes an impressive profit of $10,000 per one cent (or $0.01) of price increase:

$$1{,}000{,}000 * 0.01 = 10{,}000$$

But what if the share price trades below $8.50 in a year's time? Well, in that case, the profit turns into a no less impressive loss of $10,000 per one cent price decrease.

The symmetry of the risk profile of forwards can therefore be described as follows: if the price of the underlying goes up, the forward buyer of the underlying makes money and the forward seller loses – if the price of the underlying goes down, the forward buyer of the underlying loses money and the forward seller wins. The P&L function for both the buyer and the seller is linear:

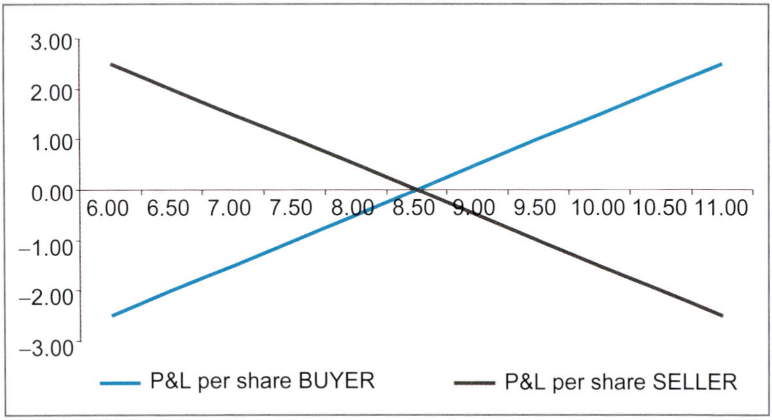

Financial options however have an asymmetric risk profile. An option is a contract which gives the buyer the right, but not the obligation, to buy or sell the underlying at a predefined price on or before a given date. The right to buy the underlying is referred to as a call option; the right to sell is a put option.

To benefit from an increase of the share price, the trader could have bought a one-year call option on Ford Motor Co. with a strike price of $8.50. In other words, the right to buy one Ford share at a price of $8.50 in a year's time. If, at that time, the price of the shares is higher than $8.50, the trader will exercise his option (i.e. he will use his right) and buy the share at the strike price. By selling the shares into the market, he then will realise his profits.

If the share price is lower than the strike, the trader would simply let his option expire worthless as the purchase of a call option does not contain the obligation to buy the shares at the unattractive price (as in case of forwards).

Options therefore clearly offer an advantage compared to the symmetrical derivatives (forwards, futures and swaps). Unfortunately, the most fundamental rule of financial markets has to be applied for options too: there is no free lunch. In other words: if there is an advantage, there has to be a disadvantage. The disadvantage of an option is that the buyer has to pay an upfront premium (in the case at hand, $0.65 per option contract).

This premium payment lowers the potential returns in case of a positive outcome but also represents the maximum loss for the option buyer.

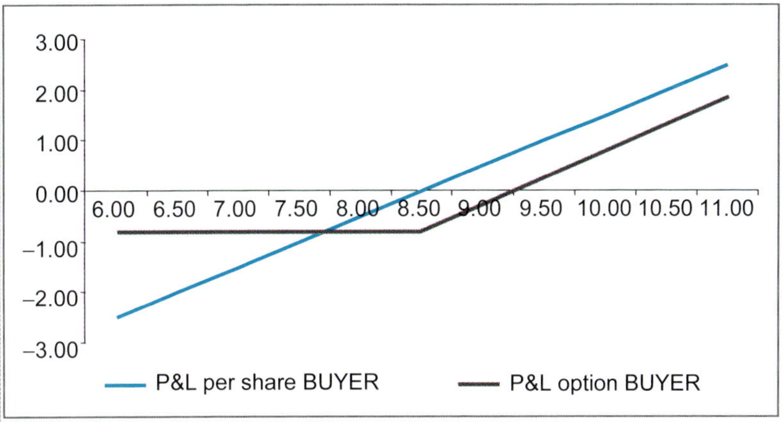

1.2 Why use derivatives?

Despite the aloofness of some famous financial market participants, the derivative markets have shown remarkable growth in recent years. Between June 1995 and June 2007, the total outstanding positions in OTC derivatives grew from 47,530 billion US dollars to 516,411 billion US dollars.[3]

Such an impressive growth suggests that there is an advantage of using derivatives over trading the underlying directly.

But what exactly are the advantages?

[3] Source: Bank for International Settlements (BIS). Including FX, interest rate, equity-linked, commodity and credit-linked contracts, adjusted for inter-dealer double-counting.

1.2.1 Derivatives increase flexibility and choice

The use of derivatives simplifies the implementation of certain risk positions. Assume a trader has a strong view that the share price for Ford Motor Co. will go down shortly. In this case, not owning any stock certainly is not enough, the trader wants to monetise his view. But how can this be achieved?

Using the spot market, one can simply sell the stock short, i.e. sell the stock without having it beforehand. If the trader is right and the stock goes down in price, he can realise a profit by buying it back at a cheaper price. The profit will be given by the difference between selling and purchase price adjusted for transaction costs.

The only problem within this strategy is the delivery obligation. Selling securities on the spot market requires delivering the securities against payment two or three days after the transaction was agreed (also referred to as t+2 and t+3 settlements). But how can we deliver a security that we do not have in the first place? The answer is quite simple: borrow it from someone else for the time you want to be short the stock.

Long-term investors usually have stocks in their portfolios without using them actively and, for a small fee, they will be happy to lend the stock to the trader for a limited period of time. The legal framework for such lending/borrowing transaction is called Global Master Securities Lending Agreement (GMSLA) and contains a very detailed regulation of security lending transactions.[4] For our purposes, a simplified illustration of the process is sufficient:

[4] The full text of the agreement can be found here:

http://www.isla.co.uk/uploadedFiles/Member_Area/General_Library/Gmsla%202009%20version.pdf

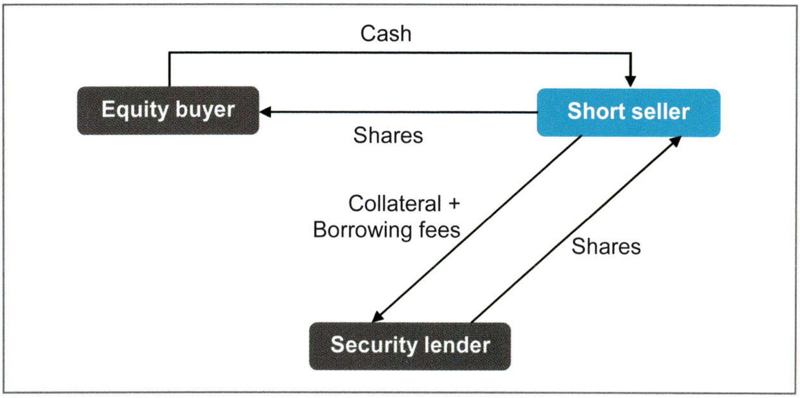

After the terms (mainly the fees) of the securities lending transaction have been agreed, the short seller receives the shares and can deliver them to the equity buyer against cash. The security lender is entitled to receive collateral – a security or cash payment pledged for the repayment of the "stock loan" and will also receive the agreed borrowing fees.

If the stock price goes down, the short seller can buy back the shares at the cheaper price, deliver them back to the security lender and receive back the collateral. If the trader is wrong and the price of the share goes up, the same principles apply but as the trader has to buy back the shares at a higher price, he will realise a loss. Generally, the performance of the trade can be calculated as follows:

$$\text{Price}_{\text{short sell}} - \text{Price}_{\text{buyback}} - \text{Borrowing fees}_{\text{per share}} - \text{Transaction costs}_{\text{per share}}$$

This short selling transaction was completely done without the use of derivatives. So how does this example show the advantage of derivative instruments?

The trader could have taken the same risk position by simply selling shares on a forward basis. This way, the shares need not be delivered in three days but, for example, in three months' time – which gives the trader enough time to buy them back in time for the delivery. Forwards therefore allow the trader to sell shares short without entering into a securities lending transaction – this is not only less time consuming but also less risky, as the potential difficulties with security lending agreements is that the lender is entitled to end the lending transaction at any time (of course by giving a sufficient notice). As it is not guaranteed that the borrower will find another party that is willing to lend the specific shares in case of an early termination by the original lender, there is a risk that he will be forced out of his short position at an unfavourable point in time and thereby being forced to buy the shares back in the open market at a higher price.

Another advantage of derivatives from the perspective of flexibility and choice is the fact that derivatives provide embedded leverage. In finance, the term 'leverage' classically stands for the use of debt to supplement investments or, in other words, use borrowed money to increase risk positions. As long as the returns on the investments are higher than the borrowing costs, this is clearly a good strategy to increase your return on equity. But why is it correct to say that derivatives provide embedded leverage?

Let us go back to our equity forward presented in Section 1.1. A trader expected the share price of Ford Motor Co. to go up. The spot market trades at $8.40 per share, the one-year forward price is $8.50. To get exposed to changes in the stock price, the trader can buy the shares spot or enter into a forward transaction. As shown earlier, the trader will make similar returns on both investment alternatives – the main difference is the funding requirement. In order to buy the shares in the spot market, the trader has to borrow $8.40 per share and this will result in interest rate payments. In the case of a forward purchase, the settlement does not happen before the end of the one-year forward period[5] and a cash borrowing is not required: the leverage is therefore embedded in the forward transaction.

---

[5] The time between spot and the forward settlement date is also referred to as the forward period.

You might now think you have found a violation of the universal no-free-lunch principle that was postulated earlier. As the use of derivatives supersedes the borrowing and therefore eliminates the borrowing costs, it looks like there is a monetary advantage of the derivative alternative. But have a look at the prices of the two alternatives: the forward price in this case is slightly higher than the spot price. In fact, borrowing costs, i.e. interest rates, are one of the main components in pricing forward contracts and other derivatives, but this will be discussed in more detail in Chapter 2. For now, it is sufficient to understand that using derivatives only supersedes the borrowing transaction; the borrowing costs, however, are incorporated in the price of the derivative contract.

1.2.2 Derivatives enable more efficient speculation

The traders we have come across in this book so far were all engaged in so-called directional trading – a simple strategy that results in a profit when the price of the underlying moves in the direction that was expected.

Sometimes, a trader has no directional view but wants to be exposed to volatility. Such a view cannot be monetised without the use of derivatives, since the purchase or the sell of an underlying will always result in a directional risk. In this case, the trader wants to be exposed to movements in the underlying price in either direction – he therefore wants to be exposed to volatility.

Let us assume a trader expects big price movements in Ford Motor Co. shares over the next year. He therefore wants to be long volatility, i.e. benefit from prices to move in either direction.[6] But how can this be achieved?

---

[6] Volatility describes the magnitude of the price move rather than the direction and refers to the amount of risk or uncertainty about the size of changes of a market price. A trading strategy that will benefit from price movements is referred to as a long volatility position. A trader is short volatility when his position would benefit from a constant price of the underlying within a certain period. Please note that volatility trades are not always set up in isolation but they can be part of more complex strategies (for example, combinations of volatility and directional trades).

As seen in Section 1.1, there is one class of derivative instruments that differs significantly from the other three. In contrast to forwards, futures and swaps, financial options have an asymmetric risk profile which means that the loss of the option buyer is limited to the premium paid. At the same time, there is significant upside potential, should the underlying price move in the right direction. Options can be used to construct volatility trades. A very simple example – probably the one the trader in our case would use – is called a straddle.

If the trader expects the share price to move but does not have a directional view, i.e. the price could go either up or down. In such a situation, the trader would buy the straddle which consists of the following option pair: a one-year call option on Ford with the strike being at the current price of $8.40 and a one-year put option on Ford with an identical strike. Assuming the trader has to pay a total premium of $1.35 per option pair, the profit and loss profile of the straddle will look as follows:

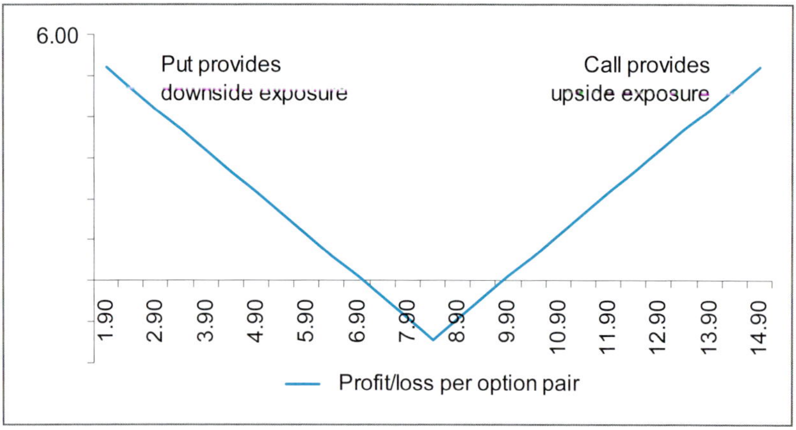

The worst case scenario for the trader is that at expiry of the options in a year's time, the price of Ford shares will still be at $8.40. In that case, none of the rights will offer any value and expire worthless; the total premium of $1.35 (the price for buying the straddle) will be lost. But as soon as the price moves away from \$8.40, one of the purchased options will offer some value: the call if the price is above \$8.40, the put if the price is below \$8.40. The breakeven prices for this strategy (i.e. the price that has to be exceeded alternatively undercut so that the trade turns out to be profitable) can be calculated like this:

$$\text{Upper breakeven} = \text{Call strike} + \$1.35 = \$8.40 + \$1.35 = \$9.75$$

$$\text{Lower breakeven} = \text{Put strike} - \$1.35 = \$8.40 - \$1.35 = \$7.05$$

At a price of \$9.75, the value of the call option compensates the total premium payment of \$1.35; at a price of \$7.05, the value of the put equalises the straddle price. If the price moves more than \$1.35 away from the current value of \$8.40, this strategy will pay a profit – if the prices moves less than \$1.35 or not at all, this trade will result in a loss which is capped at \$1.35 per option pair.

Thus, derivatives not only allow us to trade directional movements of the underlying in a much more convenient way, but they also enable us to trade price volatility directly without the involvement of any outright directional position.

However, derivatives do not only grant access to volatility as a whole new asset class, they can also increase efficiency of directional trades. Let us assume a trader expects the price of Ford shares to fall from the current price of \$8.40 but is very confident that it will not fall below \$7. The first step would be to sell the shares short (either on the spot market, which then requires a security lending transaction, or using a one-year forward contract priced at \$8.50). This results in a risk position that will benefit from a decline in share prices. But this only monetises part of the trader's view, as he does not only have an expectation about the direction but also on the magnitude of the move. To monetise the view on the magnitude of the price move, we can again use financial options.

The short position – and let us assume for simplicity the trader sold the stocks using a forward contract so that the agreed selling price is $8.50 – will profit from a decline of the share price from $8.50 all the way down to $0. So the maximum profit per share is $8.50 minus transaction costs. However, the trader expects a maximum profit of $1.50 per share (as he believes the stock will not fall below $7) and will be happy to give up any potential profit beyond that if that increases his benefits instantly.

This can be achieved by selling a one-year put option with a strike price of $7. This will result in a premium income of assumed $0.14 per option – which is adding to the profits of this trade. However, should Ford shares trade below the option strike in a year's time, the put option will be exercised and the trader has to buy the shares from the option buyer for a fixed price of $7. The maximum profit of this combined strategy (which can also be referred to as covered put writing) is therefore limited to $1.64 (maximum profit of the short sale plus option premium). The graph below clarifies the profit and loss profile of the combined strategy in comparison to an outright short sale – as long as the share price stays above $6.86 (option strike minus option premium), the covered put writing outperforms the outright short sale.

As the covered put is still a directional bet, the trader can lose a significant amount of money if the share price increases to levels above $8.64 (short sale price plus option premium).

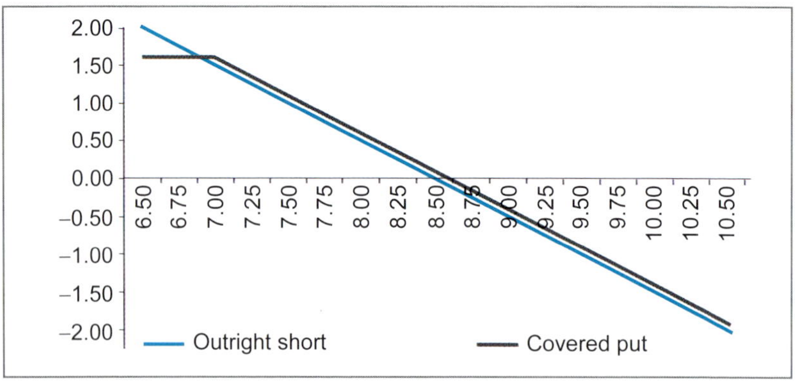

1.2.3 Derivatives can reduce hedging costs

As mentioned earlier, derivatives are not only used for speculative purposes but are also very popular hedging instruments. The term 'hedging' describes the taking of a position that will rise (fall) in value if an existing position falls (rises) in value. If the opposing price movements cancel each other out completely, the hedge is considered to be perfect. How hedging costs can be reduced by using derivatives is best explained using a concrete example.

An equity fund is currently fully invested in equities replicating the FTSE 100[7] equity index. The fund manager has the view that the non-farm payroll employment data to be published at the end of the week is going to be much weaker than expected. Consequently, he expects a sell-off in global stock markets and is therefore looking to hedge his positions for the short term. Assuming there are no limitations with regards to cash holdings of the fund, the perfect hedge would be to sell all the stocks and reinvest the cash subsequent to the expected sell-off. As the fund currently holds 102 different stocks, this would lead to at least 102 transactions and all of them will be accompanied by costs.

NYSE Euronext offers futures on the FTSE 100 index which also can be used for hedging the portfolio mentioned above. As an equity index simply represents the price level of a basket of shares (in case of the FTSE 100, a basket of 102 shares with different weightings), the index level will go down in case of the expected equity sell-off. In order to hedge his equity portfolio, the fund manager can sell the index future and buy it back at a cheaper level after share prices have gone down. This way the fund will lose money on the cash equity holdings but will make profits on the short index position. In case of a correctly calculated hedge ratio (number of index futures to be sold), the two effects will cancel each other out. Using FTSE 100 futures, the portfolio is

[7] This index is composed out of 102 shares issued by 100 companies (Royal Dutch Shell and Schroders are included with two classes of shares).

therefore hedged but – in contrast to the hedge proposed above – the fund manager only has to execute one single trade which clearly reduces the transaction costs and therewith the hedging costs.

1.3 Classification of derivatives

In the previous sections, we have already seen two ways to classify derivatives:

- Depending on the mechanics of the contract, derivatives market practitioners differentiate between forwards, futures, swaps and options
- Depending on the market place, derivatives can be classified as being either over-the-counter or exchanged-traded instruments

A third way to classify derivatives is given by the type of settlement that is provided for in the contract. Two different settlement types are possible: physical settlement and cash settlement – both types will be described in the table below.

Whereas the type of settlement for OTC trades can generally be agreed between the two counterparties, the settlement type for exchange-traded derivatives is prescribed in the contract definitions of the particular exchange.

Physical settlement	For physical settlement, the underlying is effectively delivered to the buyer on the predetermined settlement day – in return, the buyer has to pay the agreed price and hence has to raise cash. This type of settlement is favoured for hedging transaction, as given in our airline example, where the hedger has a real demand for $ in the future. However, physical settlement is no knock-out criterion for hedging transactions.

Cash settlement	For cash settlement, the underlying is not transferred to the buyer on the predetermined settlement day – the difference between the price agreed in the contract and the spot price at the delivery day is transferred as a cash payment. Cash-settled contracts do not involve any ongoing exposure post-settlement and are therefore generally preferred by traders.

Example

A trader bought Ford shares using a one-year forward contract and the forward price was agreed at $8.50. A year later, Ford shares are trading at $7.20.

In case of physical settlement, the trader now has to buy the shares from the counterpart at a price of $8.50 a share and, as a result of that, he has ongoing exposure to Ford's share price: if the stock price keeps falling, the unrealised loss will increase. To eliminate this exposure, the trader has to sell the shares in the spot market and thereby realise the to-date unrealised loss of $1.30 per share (assuming he can achieve a selling price of $7.20 and ignoring transaction costs).

In case of cash settlement, the trader simply transfers a cash payment of $1.30 per share to his counterpart. The loss is realised immediately and no further transactions are required.

Research Task

1. In late October 2008, common shares of the German car maker Volkswagen (VW) jumped from around €200 to above €1,000 within two days. Please find the answers to each of the following questions:
   - What triggered the increase in share price?
   - Why were short sellers forced to cover their positions?
   - What happened to the borrowing fees for VW shares in the securities lending market in your opinion?

2

Forward Pricing and the Cost of Carry

As mentioned earlier, forwards are tradable on various underlying asset classes. Whereas all these asset classes have specific features to be considered, there is a fundamental pricing approach that is used as the basis for all forward and futures pricing operations.

Forwards and futures can be replicated by a series of physical positions. Maybe you remember the section where we discussed the embedded leverage of derivatives: the conclusion was that buying the shares on a forward basis involves a very similar risk profile to buying the shares on the spot market – the only difference between both alternatives lies in the funding requirement for the spot purchase. We also indicated that this funding requirement is one of the major drivers for the difference in spot and forward prices. And as we will see in the following sections, interest rates (here used synonymously for funding costs) are used to price every forward contract – unaffected by the underlying asset class.

Since forwards can be replicated by a series of spot transactions, the forward price must reflect the costs of all these positions. In other words: the costs of reproducing the forward using spot trades must equal the price of the derivative. This refers back to one of the most fundamental laws in finance:

the no-arbitrage principle. According to this principle, two alternative ways to achieve identical risk profiles must have the same total price. If the two prices were different, market participants would be able to sell the more expensive alternative, to simultaneously buy the cheaper alternative and therewith to realise risk-free returns – which, according to the afore-mentioned no-free-lunch hypothesis, is impossible.

Buying the underlying right now and "carrying" it until the settlement date of the relevant forward contract should therefore lead to the same costs as buying the underlying on a forward basis. Consequently, the standard pricing formula for forwards can be written as:

Equation 1

$$\mathbf{P_{FWD} = P_{spot} + CoC}$$

where: P_{FWD} = Forward price

P_{spot} = Spot price

CoC = Cost of carry

Forwards on different asset classes only differ in the components that have to be taken into account to calculate the cost of carry. As mentioned earlier, a universal component influencing the costs of carrying a position to the forward settlement date are funding costs, i.e. interest rates. Depending on the considered asset class, there are other factors that could either add to or reduce the cost of carry.

2.1 Equity forwards

Equity forwards have already been used in the practical examples of the previous chapter. They are the legally binding agreement to buy (long forward) or to sell (short forward) a stock at a given future date at a price agreed today.

They are OTC products which can be settled physically or cash and in contrast to a physical holding of stocks, the forward buyer is neither entitled to receive any dividend payments nor to exercise any associated voting rights during the forward period.

2.1.1 Pricing

The pricing of equity forwards follows the standard procedure introduced above: the derivative is reproduced using spot transactions, the total costs of the spot transactions are calculated and these total costs are identical with the fair price for the equity forward.[8]

Alternative I:

Buy the shares on a forward basis.

Alternative II:

Buy shares in the spot market, borrow the required cash amount, receive dividends that are paid between now and the forward settlement date.

According to the no-arbitrage principle one can say:

$$\text{Price}_{\text{Alternative I}} = \text{Price}_{\text{Alternative II}}$$

Example

An institutional investor is asking for a one-year forward price for shares of Universal Display Corp. (UVD). Let us assume the company has recently announced that there won't be dividend payments in the upcoming years.

---

[8] A market maker will pay slightly less than the fair price when he buys the stock from a client (his "bid" is below the fair price) and will charge slightly more than the fair price when he sells the stock to a client (his "offer" is above the fair price). This common practice is known as the bid/offer spread.

The market maker is not willing to take any risks on that particular stock at the moment and is looking to hedge the position. The spot price for UVD shares is \$12.40 and one-year \$ interest rates are currently 5.43%.

As there are going to be no dividend payments the only cost of carry component are the funding costs. Money market rates in \$ are quoted on an ACT/360[9] basis. The one-year forward price therefore is calculated as follows:

$$
\begin{aligned}
P_{FWD} &= P_{spot} + \text{Funding costs} \\
&= \$12.40 + \left(12.40 * 5.43\% * \frac{365}{360}\right) \\
&= \$12.40 * \left(1 + 5.43\% * \frac{365}{360}\right) \\
&= \$13.0827
\end{aligned}
$$

How will the pricing change if there are dividend payments between today and the forward settlement date?

Let us now assume United Display Corp has announced a dividend of \$0.50 per share to be paid in one month's time. In this case, the cost of carrying the stock position to the forward settlement date consists of two components: the funding costs and dividends. Whereas funding costs account as costs for the spot equity buyer, dividends are clearly an income – the cost of carry is thus reduced by dividends:

$$\text{CoC} = \text{Funding costs} - \text{Dividend income}$$

[9] For more information on interest rate calculations and day count conventions please see: T. Krause *"The Interest Rate Bootcamp"* London 2008, BG Consulting Group Ltd.

Unfortunately, we cannot just subtract the dividend of $0.50 from the forward price calculated above, as that would ignore the time value of money[10]. The dividend is going to be paid in one month's time – the forward price will be paid in one year. To adjust the forward price for the dividend payment accurately, we have to subtract the one-year future value of the dividend amount that is paid in one month's time. But how can this be calculated?

Let us assume the spot date is the 16 December and the dividend payment will be made on 16 January. Using the ACT/360 day count convention, this period consists of 31 days. Let us further assume that the one-month interest rate is 5.32%. We now can calculate the future value of the dividend payment in two steps:[11]

1. Calculate the present value of $0.50 to be paid in 31 days:

$$PV = \frac{\$0.50}{\left(1 + 5.32\% * \frac{31}{360}\right)} = \$0.4977$$

2. Calculate the one-year future value of $0.4977:

$$FV = \$0.4977 * \left(1 + 5.43\% * \frac{365}{360}\right) = \$0.5251$$

The new forward price can now be calculated as follows:

$$\begin{aligned} P_{FWD} &= P_{spot} + \text{Funding costs} - \text{Dividend income} \\ &= \$13.0827 - \$0.5251 \\ &= \$12.5576 \end{aligned}$$

[10] For an in-depth discussion of time value of money, future values, present values and discounting, please see: T. Krause *"The Interest Rate Bootcamp"* London 2008, BG Consulting Group Ltd.

[11] In practice, one would use forward interest rates to solve the problem. As a consequence of how forward interest rates are calculated, the results of both ways are exactly the same and as forward interest rates will be discussed later, we will use the step-by-step approach here.

In reality, however, neither the exact dividend amount nor the exact payment date are usually known. To price the equity forward, market practitioners use estimated dividend yields for pricing purposes.

The dividend yield is calculated for the specific forward period and is based on assumptions regarding the amount and the payment date. This is an acceptable approach as companies generally aim to keep their dividend payment policy consistent over time and also to make their payments approximately at the same time every year. However, we cannot ignore completely that pricing based on such assumptions bears a certain risk, but this so-called dividend risk is discussed in more detail towards the end of this section.

Let us now assume that UVD has not announced their dividend yet but the market maker expects a dividend of \$0.50 to be paid in one month's time. We have already calculated the future value of this dividend payment of \$0.5251. In other words: if one invests \$12.40 into Universal Display Corp. today, the likely annual dividend return will be \$0.5251. This could now easily be transferred into a yield using the following formula:

$$\$0.5251 = \$12.40 * \text{Dividend yield} * \frac{365}{360}$$

$$\Rightarrow \frac{\$0.5251}{\$12.40} * \frac{360}{365} = \text{Dividend yield}$$

$$\Rightarrow \text{Dividend yield} = 4.1768\%$$

There is no universal day count convention for the dividend yield but it is advisable to use the same day count convention as used for the calculation of the funding costs. This way, the equity forward pricing formula can be standardised as follows:

Equation 2

$$P_{FWD} = P_{spot} + \left(P_{spot} * i * \frac{Days}{Basis}\right) - \left(P_{spot} * q * \frac{Days}{Basis}\right)$$
$$= P_{spot} * \left(1 + (i - q) * \frac{Days}{Basis}\right)$$

where: P_{FWD} = Forward price
P_{spot} = Spot price
i = Interest rate (per annum)
q = Dividend yield (per annum)
Days = Days until forward settlement date
Basis = Basis of the applied day count convention

Applied to our example:

$$P_{FWD} = \$12.40 * \left(1 + (5.43\% - 4.1768\%) * \frac{365}{360}\right) = \$12.5576$$

The rounded fair forward price is $12.56. If the market maker charges a bid-offer spread of 4 cents, his price quotation is 12.54/12.58.

2.1.2 Mark-to-market valuation

As every other financial instrument, contracted forward positions are continuously valued by market participants using the mark-to-market (MTM) approach. This approach measures the fair value of any financial instrument and therefore provides an overview of a portfolio's performance. The fair value of a derivative position is given by the unrealised profit or loss of the considered contract.

In the previous section, a market maker quoted a one-year forward price on UVD shares. Let us assume the institutional investor bought 100,000 shares at $12.58 on the 16 December and the market maker did not hedge his position.

On the 16 February, UVD shares trade at a level of $11.13 and a dividend of $0.50 was paid as expected on the 16 January. The decline in stock price should have a positive P&L[12] effect for the market maker, as he shorted the stock. However, as the short position has been established on a forward basis, observing a change in spot price and equating this to the performance of the forward will be inaccurate. After all, the forward price has more influencing factors than just the spot price, as we have learned.

The correct way is to re-price the forward using current market data and to compare the contracted forward price with the updated value. The idea behind this approach is that the simplest way for the market maker to hedge his position is to buy back the shares on a forward basis. Please note: as two months have elapsed we have to compare the contracted price with the current ten months' forward price.

Ten months' interest rates are at 5.30% and the period starting on 16 February to the 16 December consists of 303 days (using the ACT/360 day count convention). The dividend yield for UVD shares for the ten months' period is 0%, as the annual dividend payment was made in January and the subsequent dividend payment does not fall into the life span of the ten months' forward contract. Based on this information, the current price for the forward contract can easily be calculated:

$$P_{FWD} = \$11.13 * \left(1 + 5.30\% * \frac{303}{360}\right) = \$11.63$$

If the market maker wanted to cover his short position, he would be able to buy the shares at ten months a price of $11.63[13]. So is it right to say the performance of the market maker is $0.95 ($12.58 – $11.63)?

---

[12] The profit and loss account collects the costs, expenses and revenues of a fiscal year.

[13] Generally, the fair forward price is used for MTM valuations. A more conservative approach would be to take bid-offer spreads into account: if the market maker wants to cover his shorts, it is very likely that he will approach another market maker for forward prices. In this case, our market maker becomes a market taker and has to accept the bid-offer spread himself. The

Of course it is not, as such a calculation would again ignore the time value of money concept. Think about when the price difference will be received: even if the market maker decides to close his position right now and is able to buy the shares forward on a ten-month forward basis at a price of $11.63, the profit will not materialise as a cash flow before the maturity of both contracts. Remember: cash payments are made at the settlement date. And as we know, a cash flow that occurs at some point in the future has to be discounted, as it is the present value that matters. The current MTM value of the forward therefore is calculated as follows:

$$\frac{\$0.95}{\left(1+5.30\% * \frac{303}{360}\right)} = \$0.91$$

The calculation of the MTM value of a forward from the perspective of the forward seller can be condensed into the following formula:

Equation 3

$$MTM_{\text{Forward seller}} = \frac{P_{\text{FWD original}} - P_{\text{FWD current}}}{1 + i * \frac{\text{Days}}{\text{Basis}}}$$

where: $P_{\text{FWD original}}$ = Originally contracted forward price

$P_{\text{FWD current}}$ = Current forward price

i = Interest rate for the remaining forward period

Days = Days for the remaining forward period

Basis = Basis of the relevant day count convention

Please note: to calculate the MTM from the perspective of the forward buyer, the result simply has to be multiplied by –1.

---

achievable purchase price therefore will not be $11.63 but $11.65 (assuming the bid-offer spread for forwards on UVD shares is still 4 cents). However, for simplification purposes, we will ignore bid-offer spreads in the following.

The forward contract has performed by \$0.91, whereas the spot price over the same period has decreased by \$1.27 (from \$12.40 to \$11.13). How can we explain the relative big difference in performance of spot vs. forward position and does this difference mean the institutional investor would have lost more by buying shares in the spot market?

Right in the beginning of this section – when we defined equity forwards and talked about their characteristics – we pointed out that in contrast to a physical holding of stocks, the forward buyer is not entitled to receive dividend payments during the forward period. In our example, there was a dividend payment of \$0.50 between the trade date of the forward (16 December) and the valuation date (16 February). As a physical holder of the stocks, the investor would have lost more money on the stock performance (\$1.27) but would also have received the dividend of \$0.50 one month ago. Ignoring the at-best marginal returns of a one-month reinvestment of the received dividend, the total performance of the physical transaction can now be set with \$0.77 (\$1.27 – \$0.50).

Taking the dividend payment into account, the performance of the physical stock position suddenly looks better than the performance of the derivative, as the loss is only \$0.77 per share and not \$0.91 as on the forward. But how can the remaining difference of \$0.14 be explained?

The better part of the difference is attributed to funding costs. As mentioned earlier, forwards have an embedded leverage feature whereas the physical buyer of stocks would have to borrow the purchase price and pay funding costs for the investment period. The moment the forward was originally traded, one-year interest rates were at a level of 5.43%. If the institutional investor had purchased the stocks physically and had borrowed the required amount for one year for the two elapsed months (62 days), an interest amount of \$0.12 per share would have accrued:

$$\text{Accrued interest}_{\text{per share}} = \$12.40 * 5.43\% * \frac{62}{360} = \$0.12$$

And what about the remaining 2 cents? This is really simple: the market maker charged an additional 2 cents as spread on top of the fair price at trade inception. As we now value the trade against the fair price (also referred to as mid-market price as it lies between bid- and offer-price) and we assumed no bid-offer spread on the physical trade, the forward buyer must be 2 cents worse off than the physical buyer.

Taking dividend payment, funding costs and bid-offer spreads into account, the performance of the forward contract and of the physical transaction are nearly identical.[14]

2.1.3 Risks in equity forwards

Generally, market practitioners distinguish between market price risk and credit risk.

Market price risk has many different facets: as a direct result of how equity forwards are priced, forwards give exposure to the spot price, to interest rates and to dividend payments. For a long forward position (shares have been bought on a forward basis), the risk matrix looks as follows:[15]

[14] If you do the calculations on Excel without rounding, you will find that the accrued interest is not $0.12 but $0.1159. In other words: the performance of both transactions is not exactly the same. This results from a change in interest rates: the forward price is not only depending on the spot price but also on interest rates and dividend yields. In the present case, interest rates have gone down from 5.43% to the level of 5.30% which leads to a marginal decrease of the forward price. Technically, equity forwards come with a small amount of interest rate risk. By contrast a physical stock position does not have any sensitivity to interest rates which explains why in the case of a decrease in interest rates, the physical buyer is marginally better of.

[15] Please note that this matrix shows the performance of isolated moves. For example, if the spot price goes up and all other price-relevant factors stay stable, there will be a positive MTM value for the forward buyer.

Changing factor	Movement	MTM impact
Spot price	Up	Positive
Interest rate	Up	Positive
Dividend yield	Up	Negative
Time to settlement	Up	Positive/negative

Apart from the time to settlement, all price-relevant factors have a definite effect on the MTM value which can be understood intuitively.

- **Spot risk:** If the spot price increases and all other factors stay unchanged, the forward price increases as it is given by the sum of spot price and cost of carry. An increase in forward prices is beneficial for existing long forward positions
- **Interest rate risk:** If the interest rate goes up, the cost of carrying a physical position of stocks goes up (as funding costs increase) and an increase in the cost of carry – all other things being equal – elevates the forward price. For a long forward position, such a move results in a positive MTM impact.
- **Dividend risk:** If the dividend yield (i.e. the expected dividend to be paid during the forward period) increases, the cost of carrying a physical position decreases as dividend payments subsidise funding costs. A decrease in the cost of carry lowers forward prices which has a negative MTM impact for long forward positions
- **Time decay:** The MTM impact of a change in time to settlement – in other words, the impact of the time decay – depends on the relationship between interest rates and dividend yields. If the dividend yield is lower than the relevant interest rate, the cost of carry is positive and the forward price is above the spot price. If all other price-relevant factors stay unchanged and one day passes by, the cost of carry goes down as the positive difference between interest rates and dividend yield is

"charged" for one day less. Time decay in this case will have a negative impact on the MTM of existing long forward positions. If, however, the dividend yield is higher than the interest rate, the forward is below the spot price and the opposite effect occurs: time decay increases the forward price which is beneficial for existing long forward positions

Another type of risk that recently gained significant importance is the credit risk. Credit risk is generally defined as the potential that a counterparty will fail to meet its obligations leaving the contract partner with a financial loss.

In our example, the market maker sold shares on a forward basis to an institutional investor and with a decreasing spot price, this short forward position performed well – after two months, the market maker had unrealised profits of \$0.91 per share. On the one hand, this has a positive impact on the profit and loss account but, on the other hand, these unrealised profits are accompanied by credit risk. In case of a default of the counterparty, the settlement of the forward contract will not take place and the market maker will not receive the originally agreed \$12.58 per share. Even if the market maker decides to replace the risk position immediately by entering into another forward transaction, he will only be able to contract the new transaction at the current – much lower – forward price. In other words, the replacement of the failed counterpart will result in opportunity costs, and these costs are referred to as replacement costs.

The potential replacement costs for our example can be calculated as follows:

Equation 4

$$\text{Costs}_{\text{replacement}} = \frac{P_{\text{FWD original}} - P_{\text{FWD current}}}{1 + i * \frac{\text{Days}}{\text{Basis}}}$$

where: $P_{FWD\ original}$ = Originally contracted forward price
$P_{FWD\ current}$ = Current forward price
i = Interest rate for the remaining forward period
Days = Days for the remaining forward period
Basis = Basis of the relevant day count convention

Accordingly, the potential replacement costs and MTM values are calculated in the same way (at least if in both cases bid-offer spreads are ignored). But there is a difference in how these numbers are handled within a financial institution: whereas MTM values always matter (as the total portfolio's performance should include any realised and unrealised profits and losses), potential replacement costs are only considered if they result in a credit risk.

In case of a negative MTM value of a position (which is equivalent to unrealised losses), the potential replacement costs are negative as well. Consequently – in case of a default of the counterparty – there won't be any financial damage, so this position will be accounted for in the total credit risk with a value of zero.

2.2 Interest rate forwards

An interest rate forward can be defined as the agreement between two parties to lend/borrow money in the future at an interest rate that is agreed today. Interest rate forwards are OTC products and prior to the trade, the counterparties have to agree on:

- **The forward period:** the time between spot settlement and start of the borrowing/lending period
- **The investment period:** how long should the money be invested/borrowed for?
- **The notional amount**

In today's financial markets, interest rate forwards are probably one of the most important instruments with a very diverse user group: physically settled forwards are frequently applied by corporate clients to lock in the costs for future funding requirements, cash-settled forward contracts – like forward rate agreements – are used by all sorts of institutions for both hedging and speculative purposes.

2.2.1 Interest rate forward pricing

For pricing interest rate forwards, the same principles as for equity forwards are applied. That is to say we have to reproduce the derivative using spot transactions and apply the no-arbitrage principle to derive the implied[16] forward rate.

Example

A corporate client needs to borrow €100 million for six months starting in six months' time. As the treasurer generally expects interest rates to rise, he would like to lock in the cost of borrowing today and calls his bank to ask for a forward rate.

Let us assume we work in the loan department of the bank and answer his call: how will we fix the price for that borrowing, i.e. the interest rate?

The first thing we can do is to make a forecast of where six-month rates are going to be in six months' time and use this expectation to fix the price. Let's say that the current six-month rate is at 4%. We expect a slight increase in rates over the next six months due to inflation pressures so that our forecast

[16] A yield curve (also: term structure of interest rates) plots the interest rates versus their respective terms to maturity.

for six-month rates in six months is 4.20%. In other words: we expect to be able to borrow the money we have to lend to the client in six months at a rate of 4.20%. But should we really charge 4.20% to the client? Of course not! The main reason for the bank to pay our salary is that they expect us to make some profits – so we definitely should add a margin[17].

But simply adding a margin won't be enough because in many cases, our employer does not want us to create interest rate risk. And that's exactly what we would do by using our expectations for pricing the loan – imagine that in six months, the six-month rates have increased and the bank has to pay 4.40% for its funding. As we lent the money to the client at a rate of 4.20% plus a margin, this would mean that the margin has decreased by 20 basis points due to unexpected interest rate developments.

We have to find a way to eliminate this interest rate risk and this means that we need to fix our funding costs today. One way to lock in the costs for a six-month borrowing starting in six months from now is to borrow money for 12 months today and invest the money for the first six months:

---

[17] And this margin is not only charged to make profits, a certain part of it is charged to receive compensation for possible losses (credit margin). In the previous section, we defined credit risk as the potential that a counterparty will fail to meet its obligations leaving the contract partner with a financial loss. In case of loans, the credit risk is obvious and mainly lies in the risk that the borrower does not pay the money back. Before granting a loan, every bank therefore should assess the probability of the potential borrower to default on the loan and also the expected severity of the default (a default on a loan does not automatically mean that the lender loses 100% of the amount, as there might be a certain recovery out of disposed collateral or out of the liquidation process). A very simplified way to calculate the appropriate credit margin is to multiply the probability of default with the expected severity of default (also known as LGD: **L**oss **G**iven **D**efault). For example, if the probability of default in our example was assessed with 0.5% and the expected LGD is 60%, the appropriate credit margin would be 0.3%.

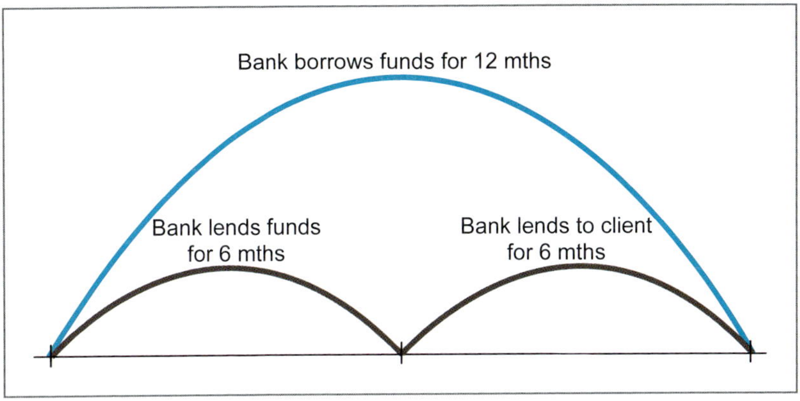

The interest rate for six months starting in six months – also referred to as the 6M6M forward rate or 6*12 (sixs twelves) forward – depends on the current 6M and 12M rate. Given the two rates below, how can we calculate the exact forward rate we should charge to the client?

Maturity	Interest rate (i)	Days in period
6M	4.00%	181
12M	4.30%	365

To answer this question, we will now come back to the no-arbitrage principle. The basic idea is that the future value – i.e. the future sum of money that will be realised by investing a certain amount of money, known as **P**resent **V**alue (PV), for a certain period and at a certain interest rate – of the following two investment alternatives must be the same:

Alternative I:

Invest money today for 12M at the current rate. The future value (FV) of €1 could be simply calculated as follows[18]:

$$FV = PV + \text{Coupon payment} = PV + PV * i_{12M} * \frac{\text{Days}}{\text{Basis}}$$

$$\Rightarrow PV * \left(1 + i_{12M} * \frac{\text{Days}}{\text{Basis}}\right)$$

$$\Rightarrow 1 * \left(1 + 4.3\% * \frac{365}{360}\right) = 1.0436$$

Alternative II:

Invest money today for 6M at the current rate and reinvest the payment that is received after 6M for the subsequent 6M at the current 6M6M forward rate. The future value in this case could be calculated as follows:

$$FV = PV + \text{Coupon on 6M investment} + \text{Coupon on reinvestment (6M6M)}$$

$$\Rightarrow [PV + (PV * \text{6M coupon} * DCF)] * (1 + \text{6M6M coupon} * DCF)$$

$$\Rightarrow [PV * (1 + \text{6M coupon} * DCF)] * (1 + \text{6M6M coupon} * DCF)$$

$$\Rightarrow \left[1 * \left(1 + 4\% * \frac{181}{360}\right)\right] * \left(1 + \text{6M6M coupon} * \frac{184}{360}\right)$$

According to the no-arbitrage principle, one can say:

$$\left(1 + 4.3\% * \frac{365}{360}\right) = \left(1 + 4\% * \frac{181}{360}\right) * \left(1 + \text{6M6M coupon} * \frac{184}{360}\right)$$

$$\Rightarrow \frac{\left(1 + 4.3\% * \frac{365}{360}\right)}{\left(1 + 4\% * \frac{181}{360}\right)} = \left(1 + \text{6M6M coupon} * \frac{184}{360}\right)$$

---

[18] The day count convention for money market rates in euros is ACT/360.

$$\Rightarrow \left[\frac{\left(1 + 4.3\% * \frac{365}{360}\right)}{\left(1 + 4\% * \frac{181}{360}\right)} - 1 \right] = 6M6M\,\text{coupon} * \frac{184}{360}$$

$$\Rightarrow \left[\frac{\left(1 + 4.3\% * \frac{365}{360}\right)}{\left(1 + 4\% * \frac{181}{360}\right)} - 1 \right] * \frac{360}{184} = 6M6M\,\text{coupon} = 4.5045\%$$

The interest rate we should charge the client for the 6M6M period is approximately 4.50% (plus the aimed margin), as this is the cost of borrowing we could lock in today using the current interest rates.

The calculation above could be condensed to the following formula[19]:

Equation 5

$$i_{fwd} = \left[\frac{\left(1 + i_l * \frac{Days_l}{Basis}\right)}{\left(1 + i_s * \frac{Days_s}{Basis}\right)} - 1 \right] * \frac{Basis}{Days_l - Days_s}$$

where:	i	= Interest rate
	days	= Number of days of period
	s	= Short period
	l	= Long period

[19] Due to the complex nature of interest rates and reinvestment risk, this formula should only be used to calculate forward rates if neither the short nor the long period exceed a term of one year (in case of annual coupon payment) or six months (in case of semi-annual coupon payments). For an in-depth analysis of reinvestment risk, coupon, zero and forward rates for longer maturities, please see: *The Interest Rate Bootcamp* by T Krause, 2008, BG Consulting Group Ltd.

This formula does not only allow us to calculate the forward rate using a set of interest rates but also allows us to examine the coherence between the shape of the yield curve and the difference between spot and forward rates.

In case of a normal yield curve (short-term interest rates lower than long-term interest rates), the forward rate is higher than the relevant spot rate. In our example, the yield curve is positive (6M spot rates are at 4%, 12M spot rates are at 4.30%) and the derived 6M6M forward rate is at 4.50%.

A yield curve is referred to as inverted when short-term rates are above long-term rates. Let us now assume that 6M rates are at 4.30% and 12M rates are at 4%:

$$\left[\frac{\left(1+4\% * \frac{365}{360}\right)}{\left(1+4.3\% * \frac{181}{360}\right)}-1\right] * \frac{360}{184}=3.6265\%$$

As we can see, an inverted yield curve leads to implied forwards[20] being lower than the spot rates and this relationship is intuitive: a market participant would only agree to invest his money long term for a rate that is below short-term rates if he expects interest rates to fall over time. For a short while (the time to maturity of the short-term investment), he loses out in comparison with a short-term investment, but if he is right and interest rates are going down, a long-term investment might turn out to be the better choice, as the original interest rate has been locked in for a longer period. Short-term investments will mature earlier and can only be reinvested at lower rates.

[20] As the forward rates are calculated from the current spot rates, they are often referred to as implied forwards – their value is implied in the shape of the yield curve.

Pricing forward rates using discount factors

For certain technical reasons, many financial institutions do not use interest rates to price forward contracts but discount factors. This allows the pricing of all interest rate linked derivatives using one set of input data (interest rate swaps and options are also priced using discount factors).

A discount factor represents the present value of one monetary unit to be paid or received at a certain point in the future. They can be used to calculate the PV of any cash flow by just multiplying the future value with the relevant discount factor, which simplifies the discounting process significantly as the discount curve has only to be calculated once and can be used to discount and price all valid instruments and cash flows.

The calculation of a discount factor generally is done as follows:

Equation 6

$$DF_n = \frac{1}{(1+z_n)^n}$$

where: DF_n = discount factor for n years (with n > 1)

z_n = zero rate for n-years

or in case of the maturity being below one year:

Equation 7

$$DF_n = \frac{1}{\left(1+z_n * \frac{Days}{Basis}\right)}$$

where: DF_n = discount factor for n years (with n < 1)

z_n = zero rate for n years

To calculate discount factors precisely and with mathematical accuracy, we have to use zero rates and not coupon rates. But using a methodology also known as bootstrapping, coupon rates can be easily transferred into zero rates.[21]

For the cases we have looked at in this section, zero and coupon rates are identical, as the maturity of none of the involved rates exceeds one year and we assume annual coupon payments. So we can apply Equation 7 and the interest rates and days as given above:

$$DF_{6M} = \frac{1}{1 + 4\% * \frac{181}{360}} = 0.980285$$

$$DF_{12M} = \frac{1}{1 + 4.30\% * \frac{365}{360}} = 0.958224$$

To calculate the forward rate using discount factors, we have to remodel Equation 5:

$$i_{fwd} = \left[\left(\frac{1 + i_l * \frac{Days_l}{Basis}}{1 + i_s * \frac{Days_s}{Basis}}\right) - 1\right] * \frac{Basis}{Days_l - Days_s}$$

$$\Rightarrow \left[\left(\frac{\frac{1}{1 + i_s * \frac{Days_s}{Basis}}}{\frac{1}{1 + i_l * \frac{Days_l}{Basis}}}\right) - 1\right] * \frac{Basis}{Days_l - Day_s}$$

$$\Rightarrow \left[\left(\frac{DF_s}{DF_l}\right) - 1\right] * \frac{Basis}{Days_l - Days_s}$$

[21] As a detailed discussion about the differences between coupon and zero rates and the concepts of bootstrapping will go beyond the scope of this book, I would like to refer you again to: *"The Interest Rate Bootcamp"*, by T Krause, BG Consulting Group Ltd.

Applied to our example, the calculation looks as follows:

$$\left[\left(\frac{0.980825}{0.958224}\right)-1\right]*\frac{360}{365-181}=4.5045\%$$

2.2.2 Forward Rate Agreements

So far, we have only looked at physically settled interest rate forward contracts. While this type of contract is popular amongst liquidity managers in corporate treasuries, for traders the involvement of cash borrowing and lending is rather unattractive. Cash borrowing and lending does incorporate credit risk on the underlying notional and that is why – as discussed earlier – credit margins are involved which makes pricing a lot more complex, as we have to apply different sets of interest rates for the borrowing leg and for the lending leg of the transaction. To neutralise this problem, cash-settled forward contracts have been developed and they are referred to as **F**orward **R**ate **A**greements (FRAs).

Technically, a FRA is the agreement to exchange a fixed rate of interest (FRA rate) for an interest rate that is determined at expiry of the FRA contract (relevant fixing of the reference rate LIBOR/EURIBOR).

LIBOR and similar interbank reference rates

LIBOR (**L**ondon **I**nter**B**ank **O**ffered **R**ate) is a widely used benchmark for money market rates and was created to meet the need of banks for a "neutral" reference rate to fix payments on various financial instruments. LIBOR can be interpreted as the rate at which banks can borrow unsecured funds in marketable size from other banks in the London interbank market. It is fixed and published daily by the British Banker Association (BBA) as a filtered average rate for maturities of one day, one week, two weeks and for one to 12 months.[22]

[22] For more information on LIBOR fixing, please see: http://www.bbalibor.com/bba/jsp/polopoly.jsp?d=1627

LIBOR is currently fixed for ten currencies but, for some of them, there are additional domestic money market fixings that are used as the standard reference rate for financial instruments denominated in the relevant currency. Interest rate derivative contracts denominated in euros for example are using EURIBOR rates. The fixing process of EURIBOR follows the same principles than LIBOR, but the fixing is done by the European Banking Federation (EBF) based in Brussels.

As FRAs are OTC instruments, the counterparties have to agree on:

- **Forward period**: time from spot until the fixing date of the reference rate
- **FRA period**: just a different expression for the investment period we have seen in connection with physically settled forwards. The FRA period is given by the maturity of the reference rate
- **Notional amount**

The nomenclature of FRAs is linked to forward period and the total covered period (i.e. the forward period plus the FRA period). A “fives elevens” (or 5*11, ${}_5f_{11}$) therefore is a FRA with a six-month rate that is fixed in five months’ time:

Although forward rate agreements are agreements to exchange interest rate payments on a given notional amount at a given point in the future – and nothing is bought nor sold – market participants are referring to the counterparties as FRA buyers and FRA sellers.

- FRA buyer: the party that pays the FRA rate and receives the future LIBOR rate. The FRA buyer therefore profits if the LIBOR fixing exceeds the FRA rate agreed at trade inception

- FRA seller: the party that pays the future LIBOR rate and receives the FRA rate. The FRA seller therefore benefits from a LIBOR fixing that is below the FRA rate agreed at trade interception

Example

A corporate client has a €100 million loan with a floating coupon of six-month EURIBOR + 2.3%. The next fixing of the coupon will take place in two months' time, the coupon period will be 184 days and the treasurer of the company believes interest rates will go up significantly. Two-month rates (59 days) are currently at 4.1502% and eight-month rates (243 days) at 4.2000%.

The market maker quotes a price for a "twos eights" FRA of 4.1775% to 4.1975% (bid-offer spread of 2 basis points around the fair forward rate of 4.1875%) and the treasurer who is exposed to a rise in six-month rates over the next two months decides to buy the FRA on the same notional as the loan. Technically, the corporate agrees to pay a fixed rate of 4.1975% (client has to cross the bid-offer spread) for a six-month period starting in two months' time and to receive the six-month EURIBOR as fixed in two months' time on the same notional amount for the same period. The corporate therefore has fixed the borrowing costs for the next coupon period at a rate of 6.4975% (4.1975% + 2.3%):

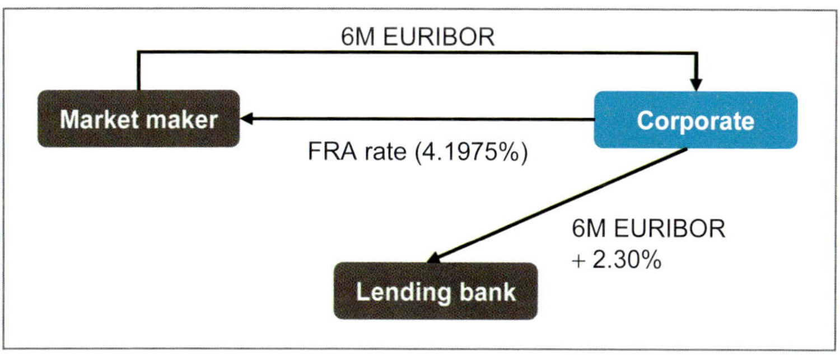

In reality however, the cash settlement works slightly different from the illustrated exchange of interest rates. To minimise credit risks, the discounted net interest payment will be transferred.

To clarify the settlement method, let us assume that two months later, the six-month EURIBOR is fixed at a rate of 4.53%. Within the FRA contract, the corporate is now entitled to receive the EURIBOR rate and to pay the FRA rate of 4.1975%. At settlement date, only one party needs to transfer a payment – to minimise transactions costs, only the net interest rate will be paid (in this case 0.3325% from the market maker to the corporate).

Interest rates are usually quoted under the convention that the payment will take place at the end of the investment period. This is also the case for EURIBOR rates and FRA rates. In other words: the net interest rate payment should be transferred at the end of the FRA period and that is to say six months after the EURIBOR has been fixed. Without any further adjustment, the corporate would now have credit risk against the market maker for the next six months, as the net payment will only be made if the market maker does not default prior to the transfer.

To minimise this risk, the standard FRA contract provides for a payment of the net interest amount at FRA expiry. As the market maker now makes the payment six months earlier, he will of course only transfer the discounted amount. To discount the relevant payment, the six-month EURIBOR fixing will be used.

The whole calculation of the discounted settlement amount can be condensed in the following formula:[23]

---

[23] To calculate the settlement amount from the seller's perspective, we just have to reverse the notation to $(i_{FRA} - i_{ref})$

Equation 8

$$DSA = \frac{(i_{ref} - i_{FRA}) * Notional * \frac{Days}{Basis}}{1 + \left(i_{ref} * \frac{Days}{Basis}\right)}$$

where: DSA = discounted settlement amount

i_{FRA} = FRA rate

i_{ref} = relevant fixing of the reference rate

Applied to our example:

$$DSA = \frac{(4.53\% - 4.1975\%) * 100{,}000{,}000 * \frac{184}{360}}{1 + \left(4.53\% * \frac{184}{360}\right)} = €166{,}098.71$$

The amount can then be used by the corporate to subsidise the increased borrowing costs of now 6.83% (4.53% + 2.3%) on the loan. But please note that the settlement amount of the FRA is received six months before the coupon payment of the loan. As a rational market participant, the treasurer will now invest this amount for the next six months and assuming a rate of 4.53% could be achieved, the future value of this amount is:

$$166{,}098.71 * \left(1 + 4.53\% * \frac{184}{360}\right) = €169{,}944.44$$

The total payment in six months' time will therefore be:

$$100{,}000{,}000 * 6.83\% * \frac{184}{360} - 169{,}944.44 = €3{,}320{,}944.44$$

And this total payment translates into an effective borrowing rate of:

$$3{,}320{,}944.44 = 100{,}000{,}000 * i * \frac{184}{360}$$

$$\Rightarrow \left(\frac{3{,}320{,}944.44}{100{,}000{,}000}\right) * \frac{360}{184} = 6.4975\%$$

2.2.3 Risks in interest rate forwards

Apart from the credit risk, which has been discussed in connection with the physically settled forward contracts, there are similar market price and credit risks (even in case of cash-settled contracts) as discussed for equity forwards in Section 2.1.3.

The generic forward pricing formula (Equation 5) shows that the cost of carry components of an interest rate forward are given by the spot rate for a maturity equal to the forward period and by the spot rate for a maturity equal to the forward period plus the investment or FRA period. FRAs and interest rate forwards are therefore sensitive to changes in interest rates.

For a market maker, it is generally not enough to know what his primary risks are but the risks also need to be quantified. The main reason for this is the fact that a market maker might not want to hedge a position, taking the opposite position in another contract, but use cheaper alternatives to create a proxy hedge. In the ideal case, of course the market maker just brokers between two clients, one being the buyer of the FRA, the other being the seller.

Let us take our previous example. The market maker quoted 4.1775% as a bid and 4.1975% as an offer. The buyer of the FRA paid 4.1975%. If, at the same time, the market maker has a seller of that particular FRA for the same notional amount, the agreed FRA rate for that transaction is 4.1775%. In this case, the market maker would lock in a profit margin of two basis points and would be able to show the following unrealised profits on his profit and loss account:

$$\frac{100{,}000{,}000 * 0.02\% * \frac{184}{360}}{1 + 4.20\% * \frac{243}{360}} = €9{,}940.41$$

This calculation is explained quickly: the nominator calculates the net interest rate margin for the FRA period. This unadjusted cash flow would theoretically be realised at the end of the FRA period so that we have to discount this payment using the current eight-month rate and the given day count of 243 days.[24]

In reality however, it is highly unlikely that the market maker will be able to trade the FRA straight through. To hedge the risk resulting from the FRA sale in the previous chapter, the market maker has the following two options:

Option I:

Buy the FRA back from another market maker. In this case however, the market maker will become a market taker and therefore has to cross the bid-offer spread himself. Assuming unchanged market prices and an identical bid-offer-spread charged by the other market maker, he will buy the FRA back at 4.1975%. As both transactions are accompanied by transactions costs, such an approach should only be the exception, as it will result in a net loss.

Option II:

Hedge the interest rate risk using other instruments.

In practice, the market maker buys and sells FRAs with different forward and FRA periods throughout the day. As a result, some of the underlying interest rate risks might offset each other. The remaining risk however will be hedged or at least monitored very closely. In either case, a detailed risk reporting is required so that the involved traders are always aware of their risk positions.

[24] As said earlier, the cash settlement of FRAs is done transferring the discounted net amount at the end of the forward period. To reflect this in the calculation, a discounting of the unadjusted net amount for six months using a two-month forward discount factor for a six-month maturity followed by a further discounting using the spot discount factor for a two-month is also possible and will lead to the same result.

The standard method to measure interest rate risk on an operational basis is the PV01[25] method. This method displays the absolute change in value of a portfolio in case of a change in interest rates. As there are different interest rates for different maturities and they do not necessarily all change in the same direction or with the same magnitude, the PV01 for a portfolio cannot be expressed as a single number but is reported as a vector.

We now want to have a look at the PV01 vector of the short position the market maker has taken in the FRA as described above (the corporate bought the FRA with a notional of €100 million). For simplification, let us assume that the trade has been done on the fair forward rate of 4.1875% and that this is the only trade the market maker has on his books (no other FRAs have been traded, no hedge has been initiated). The PV01 vector for this position would look as follows:

Maturity	PV01
1M	0.00
2M	1,640.17
3M	0.00
4M	0.00
5M	0.00
6M	0.00
7M	0.00
8M	-6,510.54

[25] PV01 stands for the present value of 1 basis point (also referred to as PVBP, DV01 (dollar value of a basis point) or BPV (basis point value).

Market convention is to calculate the PV01 values under the assumption that the underlying interest rate goes up by 1 basis point. As a result, the above table can be interpreted as follows:

- If the two-month rate increases by 1 basis point and all other rates stay unchanged the market maker will gain €1,640.17 on a mark-to-market basis (unrealised profits)
- If the eight-month rate increases by 1 basis point and all other rates stay unchanged the market maker will lose €6,510.54 on a mark-to-market basis (unrealised losses)

But how are these numbers calculated?

In case of a FRA, this is quite simple. As the implied forward rate according to Equation 5 can only be affected by a change in two-month and eight-month rates, we can assume a PV01 of zero for all other rates. For the two-month and for the eight-month rates, we will have to perform a scenario analysis.

Scenario I:

Two-month rates increased to 4.1602% (from 4.1502%); eight-month rates stable at 4.20%.

The recalculation of the forward rate leads to the following result:

$$\left[\frac{\left(1+4.2000\% * \frac{243}{360}\right)}{\left(1+4.1602\% * \frac{59}{360}\right)}-1\right] * \frac{360}{184}=4.1842\%$$

Assuming the market maker is able to close out his position at mid-market prices, the increase of 1 basis point in two-month rates will lead to a profit of[26]:

$$\frac{(4.1875\% - 4.1842\%) * 100{,}000{,}000 * \frac{184}{360}}{1 + 4.20\% * \frac{243}{360}} = €1{,}616.79$$

We have already seen this calculation when we discussed the profit and loss effect of the bid-offer spread. Since the market maker has sold the FRA, this means that he receives the FRA rate. In case of a decrease of the forward rate, the market maker can close out the short position by buying back the FRA and paying a lower FRA rate. In case of an increase of the two-month rate by 1 basis point, the forward rate would only go down marginally so that the difference in FRA rates is only 0.33 basis points.[27] This difference is used to calculate the net interest rate payment that would be made at the end of the FRA period and as this payment is eight months away, we discount the amount over 243 days using the current eight-month rate.

Scenario II:

Two-month rates stable at 4.1502%; eight-month rates increased to 4.21% (from 4.20%).

The recalculation of the forward rate leads to the following result:

$$\left[\frac{\left(1 + 4.2100\% * \frac{243}{360}\right)}{\left(1 + 4.1502\% * \frac{59}{360}\right)} - 1\right] * \frac{360}{184} = 4.2006\%$$

[26] Please note that all the following calculations have been done using spreadsheets and, therefore, there is no interim rounding.

[27] Please note that PV01 calculations are always based on a change of 1 basis point in directly observable market rates, i.e. spot rates. The calculation of the P&L effect of a change in forward rate is very unusual for risk management purposes.

Assuming the market maker is able to close out his position at mid-market prices, the increase of 1 basis point in eight-month rates will lead to a loss of:

$$\frac{(4.1875\% - 4.2007\%) * 100{,}000{,}000 * \frac{184}{360}}{1 + 4.21\% * \frac{243}{360}} = -€6{,}519.14$$

The same principles apply as in the calculation for Scenario I. The market maker is short the FRA and is therefore losing money on a mark-to-market basis if the eight-month rate, and consequently the 2*8 FRA rate, goes up. To close out the position now, he has to pay a FRA rate that is 1.32 basis points higher than the one he receives on the original position. This difference applied to the notional of 100 million over 184 days and discounted by the new eight-month rate of 4.21% for the total period of 243 days leads to the above calculated loss.

As we have seen, the change in the implied forward rate is not the same for a change in two-month rates and in eight-month rates by 1 basis point each. While the forward only reacts to a change in two-month rates by 0.33 basis points, the same increase in eight-month rates will lead to a change in forward rates of 1.32 basis points. But as we are already quite familiar with the forward formula (Equation 5), this does not come as a surprise: as the longer forward rate has a much higher weighting (given by the higher number of days it has to be applied for), the impact of a change in the longer rate on the forward rate must be greater. As a general rule, we can conclude:

The PV01 vector of a FRA shows two noteworthy sensitivities: one lies in the maturity bucket of the forward period, the other one lies in the maturity bucket of the total period (forward period + FRA period). The sensitivity to a change in the longer rate exceeds the sensitivity to a change in the shorter rate by far!

In the beginning of this section, we briefly mentioned that FRAs, although cash settled at the end of the forward period, can bear credit risk. We have already seen the reason for that when we discussed the risk on equity forwards in Section 2.1.3. Like_equity forwards, FRA contracts also bear the risk that the counterparty will fail to meet its obligations, leaving the market maker with a financial loss. The same principles as for equity forwards apply: any profits on the FRA position that have not materialised in form of a cash flow yet are at risk (potential replacement costs) and lead to an increase of credit risk against the particular counterpart.

2.2.4 FRAs and convexity

At the end of the section on interest rate forwards, let us have a quick look at a technical aspect that is applicable to most interest rate linked contracts: the convexity. In principle, convexity describes the fact that the payoff profiles of such instruments do not follow a linear line, but when plotted in a graph will show a convex shape.

Let us use the above example to clarify this. The PV01 vector showed the following sensitivities:

Maturity	PV01
2M	1,616.79
8M	–6,519.14

The simple interpretation was that the value of the short position in the 2*8 FRA will go up by €1,616.79 if two-month rates increase by 1 basis point (or will go down by €1,616.79 if the two-month rates decrease by the same magnitude) and that the value of the short FRA position will go down (up) €6,519.14 if the eight-month rate increases (decreases) by 1 basis point.

If the payoff profile of the FRA was linear, the unrealised loss of a 50bp parallel shift of the yield curve to the upside should be:

$$50 * (1{,}616.79 - 6{,}519.14) = -€245{,}117.50$$

Let us use the revaluation approach to see if this is true:

$$\left[\frac{\left(1+4.7000\%*\frac{243}{360}\right)}{\left(1+4.6502\%*\frac{59}{360}\right)}-1\right]*\frac{360}{184}=4.6803\%$$

$$\frac{(4.1875\%-4.6803\%)*100{,}000{,}000*\frac{184}{360}}{1+4.70\%*\frac{243}{360}}=-€244{,}136.85$$

As we can see, the actual loss is smaller than the one estimated using the PV01 value. But why is that?

The answer to that question lies in the denominator of the above calculation. A parallel increase of the curve leads to an increase in the relevant forward rate so that the expected payout of the FRA contract from the perspective of the market maker (FRA seller, receiver of the FRA rate and payer of the reference rate) goes negative. But the increase in the eight-month rate also has a "positive" impact: to calculate the present value of the expected negative payout, the net difference in interest rate payments is discounted back to the valuation date. As we have seen earlier, discount rates and the present value are negatively correlated (i.e. if discount rates go up, the present value of a future payment goes down) so that an increase in the eight-month rate therefore does not only lead to an increase of the relevant forward rate but also to a larger discounting effect. As a direct result, the loss does not show a linear but disproportionally small effect.

How will the payoff look for a 50bp parallel shift to the downside? Using the linear approximation, the profit for the market maker would be expected to be €245,117.50. Using our revaluation approach, the result again will be slightly different:

$$\left[\frac{\left(1+3.7000\%*\frac{243}{360}\right)}{\left(1+3.6502\%*\frac{59}{360}\right)}-1\right]*\frac{360}{184}=3.6939\%$$

$$\frac{(4.1875\% - 3.6939\%) * 100{,}000{,}000 * \frac{184}{360}}{1 + 3.70\% * \frac{243}{360}} = €246{,}144.97$$

This time, the actual number is larger than the approximation, as the expected positive payout for the market maker is discounted with a decreasing rate (i.e. the discounting effect is less severe).

We can conclude at this point that using the PV01 approach for P&L calculations with different scenarios will overestimate his losses and underestimate his profits, as the P&L profile is not a line but a convex-shaped curve. The following graphic shows the real mark-to-market values for different interest rate scenarios (the x-axis shows the assumed parallel shift of the curve) vs. the linear estimation.

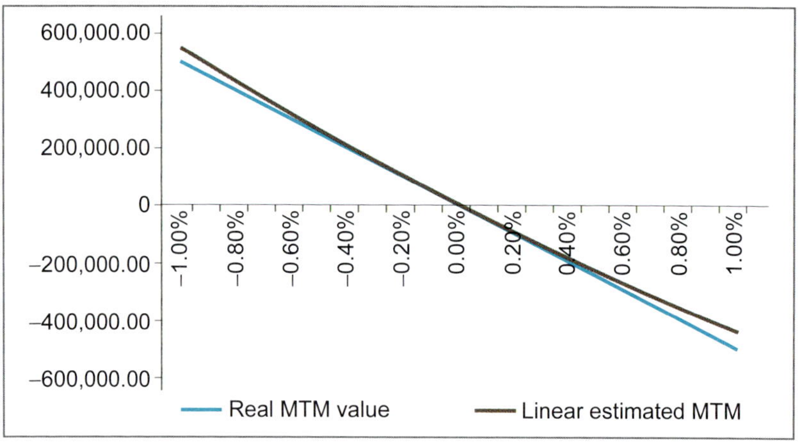

The seller of a FRA gains money more and more quickly when the curve moves down in parallel and loses money slower and slower when interest rates across all relevant maturities increase. Market practitioners refer to this profile as being long convexity – buying a FRA means being short convexity.

2.3 FX forwards

In the beginning of this book, we used the example of Air France buying five new Boeing planes to explain the principles of derivatives. The payment of US$1 billion was to be made in a year's time and to eliminate the FX risk, Air France entered into a forward contract to buy US dollars vs. euros 12-month forward. The forward FX rate was given with 1.4605.

But how can this be calculated?

As always, we have to replicate the forward trade using spot transactions and apply the no-arbitrage principle.

Air France could have used the following spot transactions to eliminate the FX risk:

1. Buy the US dollars vs. euros in the spot market (1.4600)
2. Borrow the euro amount required for delivery in 12 months and pay the relevant interest rate
3. Invest the US dollar amount received for the next 12 months and receive the relevant interest rate

The cost of carry components in case of an FX forward therefore are the interest rate of the domestic currency and the interest rate of the foreign currency. As this terminology can be somewhat confusing, we are going to use a more standardised one. Currencies are always quoted in price pairs, like in our case EUR/USD. The currency that is on the left-hand side will in the following be referred to as the primary currency and the currency that is on the right-hand side is the secondary currency. The currency markets quote the amount of secondary currency you receive for selling one unit of the primary currency (i.e. EUR/USD 1.46 means that you will receive $1.46 per € sold).

The cost of carry components of an FX forward are given by interest rates (or to be more precise: by the interest rate differential – as one rate is paid and the other received) of the primary and of the secondary currency. Let us use a concrete example to work out the FX forward pricing.

Example

Twelve-month rates in € are 1.21%, 12-month rates in $ are at 1.244%. The day count convention for both currencies is ACT/360 and applying this convention, settlement of a 12-month forward contract will take place in exactly 365 days.

Air France needs $1 billion in 12 months' time. Using spot transactions, the company would by $ spot and invest them for the next 12 months. As this investment will yield some interest, the $ amount to be purchased in the spot market is not $1 billion but the present value of it. So the first calculation has to be a simple discounting:

$$\frac{1{,}000{,}000{,}000}{1+1.244\% * \frac{365}{360}} = \$987{,}544{,}322.91$$

To have $1 billion available in 12 months' time, Air France has to buy this discounted amount and invest it at a 12-month rate of 1.244%.

To buy $987,544,322.91 in the spot market, Air France has to sell:

$$\frac{987{,}544{,}322.91}{1.4600} = €676{,}400{,}221.17$$

This amount has to be borrowed for 12 months and using a borrowing rate of 1.21%, the amount to be paid back at maturity (i.e. the future value) can be calculated as follows:

$$676{,}400{,}221.17 * \left(1+1.21\% * \frac{365}{360}\right) = €684{,}698{,}336.66$$

To conclude, one can say that Air France will pay €684,698,336.66 to receive $1,000,000,000 in 12 months' time. The implied forward exchange rate can simply be calculated by dividing the $ amount by the € amount:

$$\frac{1{,}000{,}000{,}000}{684{,}698{,}336.66} = 1.4605$$

It is quite obvious that the drivers of the forward FX price are the rates used for discounting and for compounding. A different FX rate would lead to a different € amount required for spot delivery that would lead to a different borrowing amount and to a different € amount to be paid back at maturity – which will change the result of the final calculation. A different € interest rate would lead to the future value of the € borrowing to be different which would also lead to a different implied FX forward rate.

The above calculation can be condensed into one simple formula:[28]

Equation 9

$$\text{Forward rate} = \text{Spot rate} * \frac{\left(1 + i_{\text{Secondary currency}} * \frac{\text{Days}}{\text{Basis}}\right)}{\left(1 + i_{\text{Primary currency}} * \frac{\text{Days}}{\text{Basis}}\right)}$$

[28] Please note that for accurate results in case of FX forwards with forward period exceeding one year (or six months for semi-annual coupon payments), we again would have to apply zero rates.

For our example, the calculation looks as follows:

$$\text{Forward rate} = 1.4600 * \frac{\left(1 + 1.244\% * \frac{365}{360}\right)}{\left(1 + 1.21\% * \frac{365}{360}\right)}$$

$$= 1.4600 * \frac{1.01261278}{1.012268056}$$

$$= 1.4605$$

Equation 9 allows us to analyse the relationship between interest rates in different currencies and the impact on the forward price. We have already worked out intuitively that the interest rate differential is the reason for the FX forward to trade at a different price than the FX spot. Using the formula, we can retrace this coherence mathematically.

Let us assume that 12-month rates in € and 12-month rates in $ are at identical levels of 1.21%. In this case, there is no interest rate differential – the nominator and denominator have identical values, which leads to the fraction having a value of one. The forward price is equal to the spot price:

$$\text{Forward rate} = 1.4600 * \frac{\left(1 + 1.21\% * \frac{365}{360}\right)}{\left(1 + 1.21\% * \frac{365}{360}\right)}$$

$$= 1.4600 * \frac{1.012268056}{1.012268056}$$

$$= 1.4600$$

We can also work out the coherence between the type of interest rate differential and the direction of deviation of the forward price:

- If interest rates in the primary currency are higher, the forward FX rate will be lower than the spot rate (as the denominator will have a higher value than the nominator)
- If interest rates in the primary currency are lower, the forward FX rate will be higher than the spot rate (as the nominator will have a higher value than the denominator)

2.3.1 FX swaps

In practice, FX forwards are frequently used to hedge currency risks on both upcoming payments and receivables. However, in many cases, financial institutions and multinational corporations have a different purpose for FX forwards: they use them as part of their cash management strategy.

FX swaps are a combination of an FX spot trade and an FX forward trade with both trades being agreed at the same time.[29]

Example

A EUR based company requires USD for a period of 12M to cover short-term financing needs. As the EUR accounts currently show a surplus, the treasurer decides to enter into an FX swap with a market maker rather than borrowing USD and investing the EUR amount. Assuming financing needs of $50 million, market data as given above (spot rate 1.46 and 12M interest rate in USD 1.244% and 1.21% in euros) and ignoring the bid-offer spread, the FX swap will contain the following two transactions[30]:

1. FX spot trade: The corporate buys $50 million spot at 1.46 and pays €34,246,575.34.

2. FX forward trade: The corporate agrees to sell the $50 million 12M forward at the forward price of 1.4605 and will receive €34,234,916.83.

---

[29] Please note the difference between FX swaps and cross-currency swaps. FX swaps are a combination of FX spot and FX forward trades whereas cross-currency swaps contain an initial and a final exchange of currencies but also an interim exchange of interest rate cash flows. In case of FX swaps, there is no exchange of interest rates.

[30] These two transactions are commonly referred to as the swap legs.

This kind of transaction will be referred to as: client sells and buys €.

As we can see the corporate will receive less € out of the forward trade than it pays into the spot trade. The difference of €11,658.51 can be interpreted as part of the funding costs and should therefore be expressed as a percentage rate[31]:

$$\frac{11{,}658.51}{34{,}246{,}575.34} * \frac{360}{365} = 0.034\%$$

This seems too good to be true: a corporate borrows $ for 12 months and only pays 0.034% on the equivalent amount in €.

The bad news is: it is too good to be true – of course, the company will not be able to borrow $ that cheap. But what are the additional cost components that one would expect to find?

So far, we have not taken funding costs/opportunity costs for the EUR accounts into consideration. We said earlier that the EUR account has a surplus. This will mean that the corporate does not have to borrow the EUR amount – so there are no funding costs to pay – but it also means that as the euros are now used to fund the FX swap, the corporate will not be able to invest them, which results in opportunity costs of 1.21% on an ACT/360 basis (which is the current 12M rate in €). The total funding costs therefore are given as follows:

$$0.034\% + 1.21\% = 1.244\%$$

This number should ring a bell: 1.244% is equal to the 12M interest rates in $ we used for all our calculations. Coincidence? Far from it: evidence of the no-arbitrage principle. The corporate has two alternatives to borrow USD for two months without having FX risk on the borrowing costs as illustrated below.

[31] For comparative reasons, we calculate the rate on a ACT/360 day count basis

Alternative 1:

Borrow $50,000,000 at 1.244% and simultaneously buy the required $ amount to make the interest rate payment on a forward basis, which will result in the following total payment in €:

$$\frac{50{,}000{,}000 * 1.244\% * \frac{365}{360}}{1.4605} = €431{,}797.40$$

Alternative 2:

Borrow the $ via an FX swap which will result in the following total costs in €:

$$34{,}246{,}575.34 * 1.244\% * \frac{365}{360} = €431{,}797.40$$

As expected, both alternatives lead to exactly the same total borrowing costs – to borrow $ for 12M will cost 1.244% no matter which way the funding is structured. Borrowing (or in our case not investing) the required € amount for the FX swap has an initial advantage, as funding costs are lower than in $ but this advantage will be neutralised by the disadvantage of the weakening of the $ on a forward basis.

If the borrowing costs are the same for both alternatives, why do corporates chose the more complicated way of FX swaps rather than borrowing the $ directly? The reason is that in reality the funding costs implied in the FX swap can be lower than the costs for direct funding. Remember that we ignored bid-offer spreads in our calculation. This is not accurate and as these spreads are typically much lower for FX swaps than they are for conventional cash borrowing/lending transactions, the use of FX swaps can have a cost advantage for the corporate.[32]

[32] This cost advantage is contrary to the no-arbitrage principle. However, as long as there is similar demand to borrow both involved currencies and the interest for FX swaps is not one-sided, the FX swap prices will trade in line with the fair forward rate. If there was excess

2.3.2 FX forward quotations

As a direct result of the cost advantage mentioned above, the market for FX swaps is very liquid and nowadays accounts for the majority of the daily turnover in FX forwards.

Quotation conventions for FX swaps have expanded into the outright forward markets so that there is a unique way of how prices are quoted for both instruments: market practitioners do not quote effective exchange rates but so-called swap points (also forward points), which represent the differential between the spot rate and the outright forward rate. Let us go back to our example to clarify this.

The 12M forward was calculated with 1.4605. Assuming the market maker wants to charge a bid-offer spread of 2 pips[33], his quote will be 4/6 (or spoken: 4 to 6). To be able to derive the correct forward rate, we have to know two things:

1. How are forward points scaled?
   For most major currencies, the forward points have to be divided by 10,000 before being added/subtracted to/from the spot rate (Japanese yen (JPY) and Hungarian Forints (HUF) have to be divided by 100) – but please check before trading.

---

demand for one of the involved currencies, prices would be pushed away from the fair level. This phenomenon occurred last during the credit crisis 2008/09, when the need of financial institutions to borrow $ led to a huge demand to sell and buy € on the FX swap. For further information, please refer to the BIS Quarterly Review, March 2008 page 73 and following.

[33] A pip refers to the smallest possible currency change. Currency pairs are typically quoted with 5 digits so a pip means a change of 1 in the fifth place:

EUR/USD: 1.4600	One pip equals 0.0001
EUR/HUF: 268.22	One pip equals 0.01

2. Do we have to add or subtract them?
   If the first number in the quote is smaller than the second, we add the scaled forward points. If the first number is larger, we subtract the forward points.

For our case EUR/USD, the forward points have to be divided by 10,000 and as the first number is smaller than the second, we have to add the forward points. The outright quotation therefore is 1.4604/1.4606 which means the market maker buys €1 12M forward for $1.4604 and sells €1 12M forward for $1.4606.

With these conventions, the derivation of outright forward rates from spot rates and swap points is not rocket science. However, the procedure seems to be unnecessarily complicated, so there must be a good reason for market practitioners to quote swap points rather than outright rates. And there is...

Earlier, we learned that the difference between spot and forward rates is driven by interest rate differentials. As swap points represent the differential between the spot rate and the outright forward rate, they are also mainly dependent on interest rates and largely invariant to changes in the FX spot rate. Furthermore, interest rates are generally less volatile than FX spot rates and swap points therefore change far less often than the outright forward rate. As FX swaps are primarily used for funding purposes – and the spot rate is the calculation basis for both the spot and the forward transaction – the counterparties are not very sensitive to changes in the FX spot rate and typically agree on the swap points first and set the relevant spot FX rate in a second step.

To show the relative low sensitivity with regards to the FX spot rate, let us go back to our initial FX swap example as presented in Section 2.3.1. The corporate bought and sold € at a spot rate of 1.46 and a forward rate of 1.4605; the total costs of funding were calculated with 1.244%.

Let us assume now that the counterparties have just agreed the forward points (for simplicity, bid-offer spread should once again be ignored so that the forward points are quoted as 5 (or outright 0.0005)) and the spot price jumps to 1.47. The cash flows of the FX swap now have changed:

1. FX spot trade:
   The corporate buys $50 million spot at 1.47 and pays €34,013,605.44.
2. FX forward trade:
   The corporate agrees to sell the $50 million 12M forward at the forward price of 1.4705 and will receive €34,002,040.12.

Let us recalculate the implied funding costs to see if there are any impacts for the corporate's funding costs:

$$34{,}013{,}605.44 - 34{,}002{,}040.12 = €11{,}565.32$$

$$\frac{11{,}565.32}{34{,}013{,}605.44} * \frac{360}{365} = 0.034\%$$

$$0.034\% + 1.21\% = 1.244\%$$

The funding costs are unchanged (at least, if we round to three decimal places) as the modified FX spot rate is affecting the spot and the forward transaction in the same way – there is literally no sensitivity to a change in spot rates. The risk of the corporate clearly lies in a change of interest rates and the eventual resulting increase in funding costs.

2.3.3 Risks in FX forwards

As for all other forward contracts we have discussed so far, let us now have a look at the risks from a market maker's perspective. For this, we want to concentrate on the FX forwards, as the risk profile of FX swaps has generally been discussed in the previous section.

So let us go back to our Air France example and assume that the airline just agreed to buy $1 billion 12M forward at a price of 1.4605. The EUR/USD spot trades at 1.46. 12M rates are 1.21% in € and 1.244% in $. The market maker is now contractually obliged to deliver $1 billion in 12M and will receive €684,697,021.57 for it. Let us examine the impact of a change in all three possible risk factors:

1. A change in the spot rate

   Before any hedge is executed, the $ decreases in value and the spot now trades at 1.4607. As interest rates are unchanged, the swap points will stay constant and the new outright forward rate can be calculated with 1.4612:

$$\text{Forward rate} = 1.4607 * \frac{\left(1 + 1.244\% * \frac{365}{360}\right)}{\left(1 + 1.21\% * \frac{365}{360}\right)}$$

$$= 1.4607 * \frac{1.01261278}{1.012268056}$$

$$= 1.4612$$

   The market maker is short $ on a forward basis and after the decrease, he can cover this short position at a lower price. Assuming he buys back the $ on a 12M forward basis at a price of 1.4612, the profit can be calculated as the difference in the € amount received and the € amount paid:

$$\frac{1{,}000{,}000{,}000}{1.4605} - \frac{1{,}000{,}000{,}000}{1.4612} = €328{,}009.80$$

   As this difference will not be received immediately but in 12M time, we have to discount the amount to receive the present value:

$$\frac{328{,}009.80}{\left(1 + 1.21\% * \frac{365}{360}\right)} = €324{,}034.52$$

As we can see, the market maker has significant exposure to a change in spot rates and as his basic position is short $, he benefits from a $ depreciation. To measure the sensitivity of his position for a change in spot rates, we can calculate the impact per pip (remember a pip for the EUR/USD cross was given with 0.0001):

$$\frac{\frac{1{,}000{,}000{,}000}{1.4605} - \frac{1{,}000{,}000{,}000}{1.4606}}{\left(1 + 1.21\% * \frac{365}{360}\right)} = €46{,}309.66$$

Please note that similar to the PV01 values discussed earlier, the pip value is not constant but depends on the level of the spot price:

Scenario 1:

FX spot at 1.45, increase in spot rate by 1 pip:

$$\frac{\frac{1{,}000{,}000{,}000}{1.4505} - \frac{1{,}000{,}000{,}000}{1.4506}}{\left(1 + 1.21\% * \frac{365}{360}\right)} = €46{,}950.37$$

Scenario 2:

FX spot at 1.47, increase in spot rate by 1 pip:

$$\frac{\frac{1{,}000{,}000{,}000}{1.4705} - \frac{1{,}000{,}000{,}000}{1.4706}}{\left(1 + 1.21\% * \frac{365}{360}\right)} = €45{,}681.98$$

According to these recalculations, an appreciation of $ leads to an increase in pip value whereas a depreciation of $ leads to a decrease in pip value. That is to say that the more the $ depreciates, the less the profit per pip is for the market maker, which explains why the above-calculated performance for a seven-pip depreciation (€324,034.52) is not consistent with the pip value multiplied by 7 (€324,167.62). "Borrowing" interest rate terminology, one could say the market maker is short convexity.

2. A change in 12M € rates

Before any hedge is executed, the 12M € rates increase by 1 basis point to the level of 1.22%. As the interest differential now has changed, the swap points will no longer be at a value of 5 and – although the spot has not changed – the outright forward price will be different. To calculate the P&L impact, we first have to recalculate the forward rate using Equation 9:

$$\text{Forward rate} = 1.4600 * \frac{\left(1+1.244\% * \frac{365}{360}\right)}{\left(1+1.22\% * \frac{365}{360}\right)} = 1.46035$$

The forward points have decreased from 5 to 4, which can be explained intuitively: an increase of € rates leads to a narrowing interest rate differential and, as a result, the difference between spot and forward rates (expressed by the swap points) decreases.

For the market maker who sold $ at 1.4605 on a forward basis earlier, this means that the costs for covering his short position have increased and he is faced with a mark-to-market loss:

$$\frac{\frac{1{,}000{,}000{,}000}{1.4605} - \frac{1{,}000{,}000{,}000}{1.46035}}{\left(1+1.22\% * \frac{365}{360}\right)} = -€69{,}469.43$$

The only good news from the market maker's perspective is that the higher rate leads to a bigger discounting effect, which at least marginally slows down the increase of losses when rates increase. But even with this positive convexity, an increase of 12M € rates of 1 basis point will still lead to a mark-to-market loss of €69,047.48.

3. A change in 12M $ rates

Before any hedge is executed, the 12M $ rates increase by 1 basis point to the level of 1.254%. Assuming unchanged € rates of 1.21%, this move will also change the interest rate differential which will be reflected in a change in swap points. As the interest rate differential widens, we should see an increase in swap points and therefore a positive mark-to-market effect for the market maker:

$$\text{Forward rate} = 1.4600 * \frac{\left(1+1.254\% * \frac{365}{360}\right)}{\left(1+1.21\% * \frac{365}{360}\right)} = 1.46064$$

$$\frac{\frac{1{,}000{,}000{,}000}{1.4605} - \frac{1{,}000{,}000{,}000}{1.46064}}{\left(1+1.21\% * \frac{365}{360}\right)} = €64{,}831.75$$

The above observations can be condensed in the following risk matrix for our FX forward:

Position	$ depreciation	12M € rate increase	12M $ rate increase
Short USD	Positive MTM	Negative MTM	Positive MTM
Long USD	Negative MTM	Positive MTM	Negative MTM

With regards to credit risk or counterparty risk, the same principles as for all forward contracts apply: any profits on the FX forward positions that have not materialised in form of a cash flow yet are at risk (due to potential replacement costs) and lead to an increase of credit risk against the particular counterparty.

Exercise

1. You are working as a market maker for equity forwards and are covering mining shares.

   a) Please price an equity forward using the following parameters:

Forward period:	3M (92 days)
3M rates (ACT/360):	3.20%
Dividend yield:	1.70%
Spot price:	€12
Spot date:	07/03/2010

   b) You sold 100,000 shares on a 3M forward basis at the price calculated in a). One day later, the mining company announces that this year's dividend payment will be delayed until the end of the third quarter but will be much higher than originally expected. How does the dividend yield change as a result and what does this mean for your P&L?

   c) Later that day (after the announcement regarding dividend payments), interest rates have gone down to 3.15% and the spot price has risen to €12.34. Please calculate the P&L for these changes.

2. You bought a 4*11 FRA with a notional of £250 million. Please assume that at the time of trading the 4M (120 days) rate was at 3.20% and the 11M (334 days) rate was 2.80% and you were able to lock in the mid-market rate as FRA rate.

   a) Please calculate the PV01 vector for this position and also comment on your convexity profile.

   b) At FRA expiry, 7M LIBOR is fixed at 3%. Please calculate the discounted settlement amount. Do you have to pay or will you receive the amount?

3. 6M rates in € are currently trading at 1.85% and 6M rates in £ at 1.89%, EUR/GBP spot trades at 0.87.

   a) Would you expect the 6M forward FX rate to trade below or above 0.87?

   b) Please calculate the 6M FX forward rate ignoring bid-offer spreads (assume 182 days for the 6M period).

   c) Please recalculate the forward, assuming £ rates also trading at 1.85%. How would you explain that there is a difference between spot and forward rates although interest rates in both currencies are the same?

   d) Assuming a market maker sold £ 6M forward, please complete the following risk matrix:

£ depreciation	6M £ rate increase	6M € rate increase

Research Tasks

1. Over the last couple of years the market for **N**on-**D**eliverable **F**orwards (NDFs) on currencies has grown significantly. Please make yourself familiar with the difference between classical forwards and NDFs by answering the following questions:
   - When are they used?
   - How does the settlement differ from outright forwards?
   - Which are the most liquid NDFs?
   - What is the limitation of NDFs as hedging tools for future payments in foreign currencies?

3

Futures

As we have seen earlier, there is a very close link between futures and forwards. Similar to forwards, futures are legally binding agreements between two parties, the buyer and the seller:

- To deal in the underlying commodity or security
- At a specified future date
- At a price agreed at the time of dealing

The main difference between the two instruments lies in the type of trading: forwards are generally OTC contracts whereas futures are traded on a financial exchange. This might seem to be a minor difference on first sight but it leads to a multitude of special features of the futures market that we – as market practitioners – have to be familiar with. We therefore start this chapter with a direct comparison of the most important features of forwards and futures before exploring equity and interest rate futures in more detail.

3.1 Forwards vs. futures

The first difference that should be pointed out is not only valid for the comparison of futures and forwards but is a general discrepancy between OTC and exchange-traded instruments.

In case of OTC instruments, the investor gets in contact with a market maker who is committed to quote two-way prices for the relevant instrument during normal trading hours for a marketable size. The difference between the transacted price and the fair price (as we have calculated earlier for equity, interest rate and FX forwards) can be interpreted as a service charge: the market maker enters into a risk position because of the investor's demand for a particular financial instrument – or in other words: the market maker provides liquidity.

As we have mentioned earlier, the contract details for OTC deals are freely negotiable: the investor can ask for the price of an 11-day equity forward, a 3.3*9.7 FRA or a 63-day FX forward and, under normal market circumstances, is very likely to receive a quote. Surely, the bid-offer spread will be a little bit wider than the spread for usual or standard contracts (e.g. 3*9 FRA), since broken maturities are a little more difficult to hedge, but there will still be a two-way price.

In case of futures contracts, the situation is slightly different. Strictly speaking, the exchange only matches supply and demand: if an investor has an interest to buy a certain futures contract at a given price, he places an order and only then, if there is a match (i.e. another market participant placed an order to sell the same futures contract at the same price), will the trade be executed.

Market participants will therefore only use futures if there is an adequate liquidity and market depth, i.e. it is possible to open or close a position with a marketable size at a fair price during normal trading hours. To assure this – even without the existence of market makers – the exchanges limit the number of different futures contracts that can be traded. As a result, market participants focus their trading activities on a small number of contracts which concentrates the liquidity and this is essential for the success of a futures contract. If there is no sufficient liquidity and opening/closing of normally sized positions can be proved to be difficult or impossible, the futures contract will not be used by market practitioners and, sooner or later, the exchange will decide to drop it.

While this contract limitation (also referred to as contract standardisation) increases liquidity, it bears a major disadvantage: the choice of contracts is limited and investors might not find exactly what they want or need.

Example

An investor wants to buy 50 Telefónica shares 12M forward and is looking at futures contracts. Equity futures on Telefónica are traded on NYSE Euronext in London in the form of "Universal Stock Futures Contracts on continental European shares". These contracts are standardised as follows:[34]

Contract size	One contract normally represents 100 shares; Italian contracts normally represent 1,000 shares. Due to adjustments for corporate actions, some contracts may have non-standard sizes.
Expiry months	Contracts are available for nearest two of the IMM[35] months (March, June, September, December) and the nearest two serial months (serial contracts expire in months other than those in the March, June, September, and December quarterly cycles). This way the next three calendar months are always available for trading.
Quotation	Euros per share, Sweden SEK per share, Switzerland CHF per share.

[34] The complete contract description can be found here: http://www.euronext.com/trader/contractspecifications/wide/contractSpecifications-3111-EN.html?docid=47433

[35] International Monetary Market, one of the three divisions of the CME. IMM months are four quarterly months (March, June, September, December) that most futures use as expiry months.

Last trading day	The last trading day is the third Friday of the delivery months (in Italy, the business day immediately preceding the third Friday of the delivery month).
Settlement	Settlement of the contracts is carried out in cash on the first business day following the last trading day (in Italy, two business days after the last trading day).

The futures contract is unsuitable for the investor for two reasons:

1. The contract size does not meet the investor's needs. If an investor is looking to buy only 50 shares but the contract size is standardised to 100, the purchase via futures is impossible as futures can only be traded in multiples of 1.[36]

2. The longest available futures contract will expire in 3M but the investor is looking for a forward period of 12M. If the investor wants to stick to futures – rather than investing into an OTC contract – he will have to roll his contracts on a regular basis. In our example, the investor could buy the current 3M contract today and sell it on or before the last trading day to buy the subsequent three-month contract and repeat this process two more times. This method allows the investor to use futures even for a 12M investment horizon but it bears a few problems itself:
   - The higher number of necessary transactions will lead to a significant increase in transaction costs
   - The rolling transaction itself can be risky (for example, the share price increases after the first futures contract has been sold but before the second futures contract has been bought)

[36] In reality, this problem will be somewhat defused, as institutional investors generally look for bigger trading volumes than 50 shares.

- The 3M futures prices are based on 3M interest rates and 3M dividend yields. As these parameters are not known in advance, the final purchase price will only be known by the investor after the last rolling transaction has been executed. Within an OTC contract, the final purchase price will be known the moment the deal has been agreed and will not depend on future interest rates or changes in dividend expectations

---

Having said that, futures contracts look clearly disadvantageous compared to OTC forwards. However, the fact that futures markets still exist and trade very actively clearly shows that there must also be some advantages.

The first advantage of futures has already been mentioned: due to the limitation of choice in contract, the liquidity for futures contracts is potentially very high. As higher liquidity also means lower bid-offer spreads, established futures markets give market participants the opportunity to trade relatively large volumes at competitive prices in a very short period of time. Especially for big trading accounts, this advantage is very weighty as speed and cost efficiency are emerging more and more as critical success factors.

Another advantage of futures is the fact that there is a central market price that is easily observable. This becomes incredibly important within the end of day valuation process. Let us assume the investor mentioned above decided to buy one 3M futures contract on Telefónica this morning at a price of €19.15 (contract details as described above) and this evening, the futures market closed at a price of €19.21. As the futures price is quoted in € per share and the contract size is 100 shares, the P&L for that day can simply be calculated as follows:

$$100 * (19.21 - 19.15) = 100 * 0.06 = €6$$

Let us now assume the investor bought 100 Telefónica shares on a 12M forward basis via an OTC transaction and the agreed forward price is €19.40.

To calculate the P&L at the end of the day, we also have to compare the contracted forward price (€19.40) with the current forward price – but as the forward is an OTC instrument, the current price is not publicly readily available. The only way to calculate the performance of the trade for the day is to re-price the forward contract using the current Telefónica spot price and the current 12M interest rates and dividend yields. We have learned how to do this earlier so that such a calculation for us is now a simple task. However, it is still a bit more time consuming than the calculation for futures. In addition to that, the relevant interest rates and dividend yields that we have to use in our pricing formula will not be explicitly given to us in practice. To find the appropriate interest rate is probably no big deal, but where can we find the dividend yield the market is currently using to price our forward? This can cause problems, as the use of a "wrong" dividend yield will lead to a wrong valuation price.

The biggest advantage of futures in comparison to forwards is the fact that an investment in futures does not contain credit risk. This benefit was the main reason for futures markets being relatively unaffected by the credit crisis – at least in terms of liquidity – whereas OTC markets, due to concerns about the credit quality of counterparties, saw some more or less severe disruptions.

As extensively discussed in the previous chapter, credit risk is inherent to every forward contract and therefore also to exchange-traded forwards. However, futures exchanges generally implement margin systems to eliminate the counterparty risk for the user of the relevant contract. The precise design of these systems is exchange specific and therefore cannot be discussed in a great amount of detail here – but the margin systems of all major exchanges consist of two building blocks:

1. **Initial margin**

- Money that a futures buyer/seller has to deposit with the exchange before trading can begin
- The amount of initial margin can vary depending on the underlying commodity and is mainly driven by its potential intraday volatility

2. Variation margin

- Money that is credited/debited to futures buyer/seller if the futures price moves favourably/unfavourably
- The variation margin is calculated every evening using the closing price of the futures contract
- Variation margin has to be paid before the next trading session begins

Let us use a concrete example to outline the principles of margining systems. Our investor bought one futures contract on Telefónica at a price of €19.15. In the evening, the closing price for the futures is set with €19.21 and the investor has an unrealised profit of €0.06 per share or €6 per contract.

Although the exchange only matches orders and never enters a risk position itself, the exchange technically becomes counterpart of both the futures buyer and futures seller:

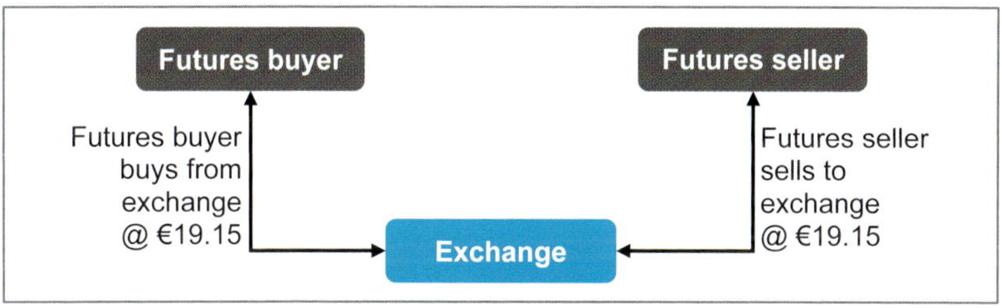

This way, the counterparty risk of our investor refers to the exchange and not to the original seller of the contract whose identity is not known by the futures buyer. The variation margin eliminates this risk: the unrealised profit of €6 is transferred from the exchange to the account of the futures buyer. The exchange itself has credit risk against the futures seller and collects a payment from this counterparty in order to cover the default risk:

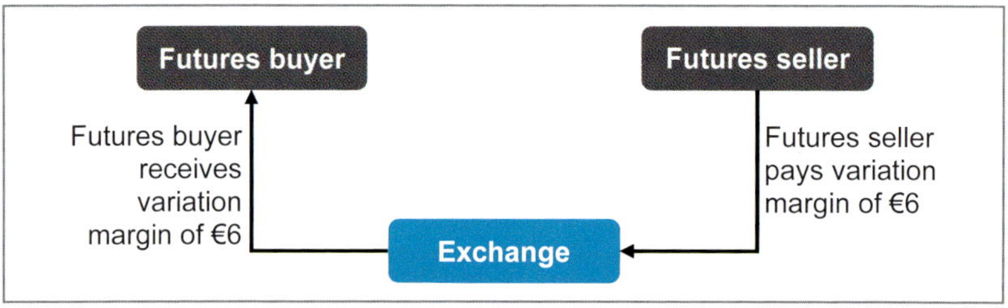

Variation margins therefore cover the default risk that results from a change of the futures price since the last variation margin payment (usually the previous working day) or the futures purchase price (if the futures contract has been traded between the last variation margin payment and the current point in time). In our example, the futures contract was bought on the day of the variation margin calculation and we therefore have to use the purchase price as benchmark. On the following day – assuming the futures contract will not be closed out – the variation margin will be calculated as the difference between €19.21 and the futures closing price of the day.

Per definition, the variation margin will not cover the price moves following a default of one of the counterparties. As the exchange acts as a guarantor for variation margin payments, any default of a counterparty before the payable variation margin has been transferred will result in a financial loss for the exchange. Hence, the introduction of the initial margin: a deposit made by futures buyers/sellers when opening a position.

However, the initial margin only provides a certain safety net, as it is usually a lot lower than the potential total losses. In our case, the initial margin is €45 per contract which can be translated into a move in share price of €0.45. Considering the initial margin payment and assuming both counterparties – futures buyer and futures seller – are opening a new position, the trade flows can be represented as follows:

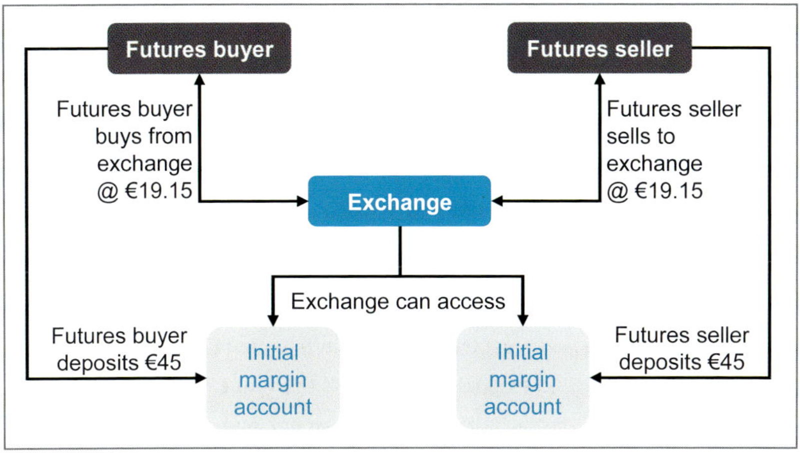

Let us assume that on the following workday, the share price of Telefónica increases further and closes at €19.66. If the futures seller defaults prior to the daily margin payments, the variation margin that has to be paid to the futures buyer, but no longer receivable from the futures seller, will be covered by the initial margin previously deposited by the defaulting counterpart:

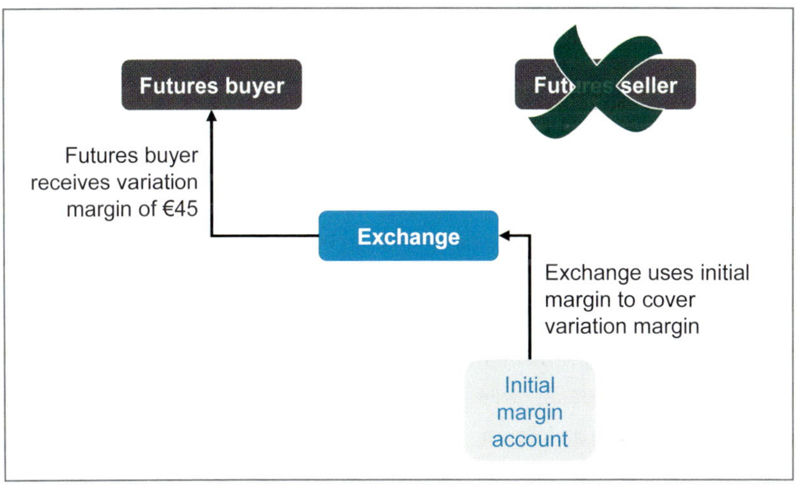

As mentioned earlier, this initial margin system offers only limited protection, as Telefónica shares can move by more than €0.45 per share and in such a case, the deposit will not be sufficient to cover the variation margin to be paid to the futures buyer. To prevent a default – and as a result, overwhelming losses – there are further protection mechanisms in place (e.g. intraday margin calls in case of unusually big price moves, default funds to cover potential losses exceeding the initial margin) and, typically, the initial margin is regularly adjusted to reflect current market volatility, i.e. in times of high volatility, initial margins tend to increase and vice versa.

But why do the exchanges not simply set the initial margin much higher?

In the very first part of this book, we discussed the advantages of derivatives and identified the embedded leverage feature as a key driver for the success of derivatives. The initial margin however reduces the leverage effect, as a certain amount of money has to be deposited at the moment of trading. To maintain the attraction of futures contracts for market participants, the exchanges try to keep the initial margin requirements to a minimum whilst simultaneously keeping the protection level of the safety net at appropriate levels. In case of open positions in different futures contracts that are traded at the same exchange, the total initial margin requirement is calculated using state of the art risk management techniques, which include correlations and other statistical measures.[37]

[37] The exchanges (or to be precise: the relevant clearing houses) provide an extensive range of information about their calculation approaches. To have a more detailed look at the applied methods, please visit the relevant websites.

3.2 Stock index futures

Although there is a wide range of futures on single stocks and the liquidity for some of these contracts exceeds acceptable levels, the futures on equity indices in most markets are still the most important contracts.

An equity index is a hypothetical basket of equities representing a particular market or just a certain portion of it. The price of this basket is reflected by the index level so that changes in share prices lead to a change in index values. Equity indices therefore allow the simple measurement of returns for a given universe of stocks and are often used by market practitioners to benchmark returns of their individual equity portfolios.

As equity indices often have regional constraints, they can be used to compare equity returns of different markets, e.g. performance of the US and the UK stock markets using the S&P 500 and the FTSE 100 indices. However, each index has its very own calculation methodology, so care must be taken in comparing index returns.

3.2.1 Price vs. market capitalisation weighting

As mentioned earlier, an equity index represents a basket of shares. To calculate the index level using the prices of single stocks, there are three main approaches:

1. Equal weighting of index members
2. Price weighting of index members
3. Market capitalisation weighting of index members

Whereas the equal weighting is not of great importance, both price weightings and market cap weightings are used amongst the most important equity indices:

DJIA	30 large US companies ■ *Price-weighted index* ■ Dividends are not included
S&P 500	500 large US companies ■ *Market capitalisation* (value) weighted index ■ Dividends are not included
Nikkei 225	Largest Japanese firms ■ *Price-weighted index* ■ Dividends are not included
FTSE 100	Largest British companies 100 index ■ *Market capitalisation* (value) weighted index ■ Dividends are not includes
DAX 30	Largest 30 German companies ■ *Total Return* index ■ Includes capital gains, dividends, mergers, etc.

In a price-weighted index, stocks with a higher price receive a larger weighting in the computations than stocks with a lower price. The index members change infrequently and changes usually only occur as a result of corporate actions. Dividend payments are generally not included within the index calculations.

Probably the best known equity index (and the second oldest US market index) is the Dow Jones Industrial Average (DJIA). It was invented by Charles Dow in 1896 and contains 30 significant stocks traded on the NYSE and the NASDAQ. The Dow is a price-weighted index and is computed by adding the share prices of the 30 stocks comprising the index and dividing by the DJIA divisor:

Equation 10

$$DJIA = \frac{\sum_{i=1}^{30} P_i}{Divisor}$$

where: P_i = Price of stock i

The index divisor is a computed number that keeps the index unchanged in the event of corporate actions or change of constituent members.

Example

Let us assume the DJIA currently has a level of 10,416 and a current index member, whose shares trade at a price of $35, has now been replaced by a new company with a share price of $65. Let us also assume that the simple sum of the constituent's share prices before the replacement was $1,293 and the divisor had a value of 0.124136. The new divisor is calculated rearranging Equation 10.

Index calculation before replacement:

$$DJIA = \frac{1,293}{0.124136} = 10,416$$

Sum of constituents share prices after replacement:

$$1,293 - 35 + 65 = 1,323$$

Theoretical index level after replacement:

$$DJIA = \frac{1,323}{0.124136} = 10,657.67$$

To keep the index value unchanged, a new divisor is calculated as follows:

$$Divisor = \frac{\sum_{i=1}^{30} P_i}{\text{Index value before replacment}} = \frac{1,323}{10,416} = 0.127016$$

Adjusting the divisor to 0.127016 will keep the index at an identical level. This method ensures that there are no jumps in index value in case of a replacement of one or more index members.

The most commonly used benchmark for the US stock market however is the S&P 500 index which aims to represent the US large cap equity market and contains 500 stocks. The companies included are chosen by an index committee by market capitalisation, liquidity, industry, etc.

The index value itself is market cap weighted and can be calculated using the following formula:

Equation 11

$$\text{S\&P 500} = \frac{\sum_{i=1}^{500} N_i * P_i}{\text{Divisor}}$$

where: N_i = number of shares outstanding for company i

P_i = price of stock i

The divisor is calculated applying the same principles as used for the DJIA and "…is adjusted such that the index value at an instant just prior to a change in base capital equals the index value at an instant immediately following that change."[38]

Let us have a look at a concrete example to examine the difference in index returns depending on price weighting and market capitalisation weighting

[38] For more detailed information please see:
http://www.standardandpoors.com/indices/sp-500/en/us/?indexId=spusa-500-usduf--p-us-l--

respectively. To keep the example clear, we will create two indices with only four constituents and the following starting values:

Stock	Price	Number of outstanding shares	Mrkt. Capitalisation
A	450	5,000,000	2,250,000,000
B	380	5,000,000	1,900,000,000
C	620	15,000,000	9,300,000,000
D	220	55,000,000	12,100,000,000
$\sum$	1670		25,550,000,000

To set the initial index values to 100, the following divisors are used[39]:

$$\text{Divisor}_{\text{price weighting}} = \frac{1{,}670}{100} = 16.7$$

$$\text{Divisor}_{\text{market cap weighting}} = \frac{25{,}550{,}000{,}000}{100} = 255{,}500{,}000$$

One day later, the market data has changed as follows:

Stock	Price	Number of outstanding shares	Mrkt. Capitalisation
A	480	5,000,000	2,400,000,000
B	415	5,000,000	2,075,000,000
C	660	15,000,000	9,900,000,000
D	225	55,000,000	12,375,000,000
$\sum$	1780		26,750,000,000

[39] The values are calculated using Equation 10 and Equation 11 respectively.

Using the updated market prices, the indices can now be recalculated as follows:

$$\text{Index}_{\text{price weighting}} = \frac{1{,}780}{16.7} = 106.59$$

$$\text{Index}_{\text{market cap weighting}} = \frac{26{,}750{,}000{,}000}{255{,}500{,}000} = 104.70$$

Although the prices for the index members in both cases have changed by the same price amount, the index values show a significant difference in price development.

How can the underperformance of the market cap weighted index be explained?

The main driver is the relative weak performance of Stock D. The following table shows the initial relative market capitalisation and the relative stock price change for all index members:

Stock	Relative market capitalisation	Relative stock price change
A	8.81%	6.67%
B	7.44%	9.21%
C	36.40%	6.45%
D	47.36%	2.27%

The stock with the largest market capitalisation has the lowest % change: Stock D represents 47.36% of the total market cap but only changed by 2.27% and therefore slowed down the increase of the market cap index.

At the same time, the stock with the highest price (and therefore with the highest weighting in the price-weighted index) has shown a relatively strong performance with 6.45%, which results in the better performance of the price-weighted index.

But type of weighting is not the only way in which the construction of the various equity indices can differ. Equity investments generally have two sources of income: stock price performance and dividend returns. The presented indices (DJIA and S&P 500) are price return indices and are therefore not including dividends in their calculation: if an index member pays dividends (or more precisely: the stock of the index member goes ex-dividend) and the relevant stock price drops as a consequence, the index will be negatively affected.

Other indices (for example, the DAX and CAC 40) are so-called total return indices: they take dividend income into account by virtually reinvesting the dividend income in shares of the dividend paying company. Total return indices therefore measure the income of an equity basket including returns on reinvested dividends; price return indices measure the pure price development of a basket of shares. Assuming identical stock price performances for both baskets over time, the total return index therefore should outperform the price return index.

3.2.2 Stock index futures mechanics

According to our initial definition of futures, stock index futures are exchange traded forwards on equity indices. The buyer of such a futures contract agrees to buy the underlying index at a specified future date and a price agreed at the time of trading. As the relevant index physically does not exist but only represents the price of a basket of shares with different weightings, stock index futures are usually cash settled. The settlement is carried out against a specially calculated settlement price[40], the procedures of how to calculate this settlement price are set within the contract definitions.

[40] Commonly referred to as the EDSP (Exchange Delivery Settlement Price).

As a direct result of the benchmark characteristics of the underlying indices, stock index futures are frequently used by a wide range of institutional investors to speculate on future price moves of the equity market, hedge the risks of their existing equity portfolios or to quickly redistribute the risk from one equity market to another. Let us use concrete examples to clarify the use of stock index futures.

Example

An institutional investor, whose $800 million assets under management are currently fully invested in government bonds, decides to temporarily switch 20% of his portfolio into the US equity market. As he is generally bullish on stocks and only has limited expertise on stock valuation, he decides against stock picking and wants to buy the diversified S&P 500 index to get a broad-based exposure. As the position presumably will only be a short-term investment, the investor decides to use futures and not to buy 500 shares in different weightings, to minimise the transaction costs.

The required amount of futures can be calculated using the data given in the contract definition issued by the Chicago Mercantile Exchange (CME):[41]

Contract size	S&P 500 futures price * $250
Expiry months	For open outcry, there are eight contracts available, the expiry months follow the March quarterly cycle (March, June, September, December). For electronic trading (via Globex), contracts are only available for the nearest expiry month of the March quarterly cycle.

[41] The full contract details can be found here:
http://www.cmegroup.com/trading/equity-index/us-index/sandp-500_contract_specifications.html

Quotation	Index points
Last trading day	The last trading day is the Thursday prior to the third Friday of the expiry month for open outcry. On Globex, the official rollover date (eight trading days prior to the last trading day of open outcry) marks the day on which the current index future is replaced by the following contract (that has been solely traded on open outcry before), as only the leading contract is traded on Globex.
Settlement	Settlement of the contracts is carried out in cash to the Special Opening Quotation (SOQ) on Friday a.m. of the S&P 500 Index.

The contract size of the futures is defined as the futures price multiplied by $250. Assuming the first available futures contract trades at 1,130 index points, the contract value therefore is:

$$1{,}130 * \$250 = \$282{,}500$$

The investor plans to invest $160 million (20% of $800 million), so he has to buy the following number of futures contracts:

$$\frac{\$160{,}000{,}000}{\$282{,}500} = 566.37$$

As futures can only be traded in multiples of 1, the investor buys 566 contracts at an index level of 1,130.

? Has he really invested $160 million in equities?

Yes and no! One of the benefits of derivatives was the embedded leverage feature, as discussed in the previous section; a futures buyer has to pay an initial margin although this initial margin is much smaller than the notional to be traded.[42] So technically speaking, the $160 million are not invested in the US stock market. On the other hand, the investor is now long 566 contracts of the S&P 500 futures and this risk position may very well result in variation margin payments and finally profits or losses if stock prices move. If the amount of future contracts has been calculated correctly, the P&L effect of the futures should be equal to the effect of a corresponding cash investment in equities. To prove this statement, let us assume that at the end of the day, the futures is trading up at 1,135. What would be the P&L effect for a real cash investment and what is the P&L effect of the futures position?

Cash investment:

The index value has increased by roughly 0.4425%, which means the value of the underlying basket of shares has gone up by the same percentage rate. A cash investment of $160 million therefore would have gone up in value by $708,000.

Futures investment:

The futures contract has also increased by 0.4425% or – using a unit of account that will simplify the P&L calculations – by 5 index points. How can we now calculate the P&L of the futures position?

We know that the contract value of a futures is calculated by multiplying the futures level with $250 – therefore, we can say that the value of one index point is $250 per futures contract. As the index has increased by 5 points, the profits for the futures position are calculated as follows:

$$\$250 * 566 * 5 = \$707{,}500$$

As the difference of $500 can be explained by the rounding the number of contracts, it is very tempting to say that an investment via futures gives the same risk than a cash investment in equities.

---

[42] For the purpose of simplification, the initial margin payment will be ignored in the following calculations.

But this certainly would be too simple! In the above calculation, we implicitly assumed that cash index and futures price are trading at the same level of 1,130 at trade inception and increase by 5 index points each. In practice, this will hardly ever be the case. Remember how we defined index futures earlier: stock index futures are exchange-traded forwards on equity indices. And in the very beginning of this book, we have learned that spot and forward prices are usually not the same, but that there is a formulistic relationship given by the cost of carry.

The price of an equity future therefore should be equal to the spot price of the underlying equity basket plus the cost of carry. It stands to reason that for pricing a forward on a basket of stocks, we can use the same formula as for pricing a forward on a single stock. Consequently, we can use the following equation to calculate the fair price for stock index futures (at least, for the price return indices):

Equation 12

$$P_{Futures} = P_{Index\ spot} * \left(1 + (i - q) * \frac{Days}{Basis}\right)$$

where:

	$P_{Futures}$	=	Futures price
	$P_{Index\ spot}$	=	Spot price
	i	=	Interest rate (per annum)
	q	=	Dividend yield of the index basket (per annum)
	Days	=	Days until forward settlement date
	Basis	=	Basis of the applied day count convention

The equation clarifies that the value of a futures position is not only affected by a change in the spot index but also by a change of interest rates and/or dividend expectations. Under normal market circumstances, however, interest rate and dividend risks are comparatively insignificant and are outweighed by the benefit of much lower transaction costs using futures.

But futures are not only used to set up speculative positions, they are also popular hedging instruments. Let us assume that an equity portfolio manager is invested in 50 companies that are all index members of the S&P 500. He is concerned that there will be a technical correction in the stock market soon and therefore wants to temporarily hedge his positions. For those who are not yet familiar with the term: hedging is the taking of a position that will rise (fall) in value and offset a fall (rise) in the value of an existing position. In our case, the portfolio manager is looking to enter into a position that gains in value in case of the expected sell-off in the equity markets to offset any losses on the stock portfolio.

The perfect hedge would of course be to sell the 50 stocks the portfolio is invested in. However, this would result in significant transaction costs and as all of the shares are represented in the S&P 500 index, the use of index futures might be beneficial. The portfolio manager should sell futures contracts and buy them back at a cheaper price when shares have sold off. To calculate the number of futures that have to be sold (also referred to as the hedge ratio), we can use the following formula:

Equation 13

$$\textbf{Hedge ratio} = \frac{\textbf{Current portfolio value}}{\textbf{Futures price * \$250}}$$

Assuming a portfolio value of $200 million and a futures price of 1,130, the portfolio manager theoretically has to sell 708 contracts. In reality however, this number often will be adjusted by the so-called beta factor.

Calculating the hedge ratio as given above ignores the fact that an independent portfolio consisting of 50 shares will not necessarily behave in the same manner as the index consisting of 500 shares. In fact, there are stocks that typically move more than the index and there are stocks that typically move less than the index. Hedging a portfolio that does not represent the index completely with an index-linked instrument (like the S&P 500 futures) leads to the risk that the returns of the futures hedge might not cover the losses of the portfolio – this scenario gets even more likely if the portfolio consists of shares that predominantly move more than the index.

The beta factor tries to address this problem. Beta is also referred to as **financial elasticity** and is a measure of the sensitivity of the return of a single asset (single stock) to market returns (the return of the index). Within the calculation of beta, both direction and magnitude are taken into account so that beta combines volatility and correlation. Technically, the calculation of beta is based on the covariance between the rates of return of the single stock and the index but, for simplicity, let us focus on the interpretation rather than the calculation of beta:

- Beta = 1: the stock moves in line with the market
- Beta = 2: the stock moves twice as much as the market
- Beta = 0.5: the stock moves half as much as the market

How can beta be used to improve the quality of the hedge above?

We first have to calculate the weighted average beta of the portfolio that is to be hedged. This weighted average can simply be calculated as follows:

Equation 14

$$\text{Portfolio beta}_{\text{weighted average}} = \frac{\sum_{i=1}^{50} N_i * P_i * \beta_i}{\text{Current portfolio value}}$$

where: N_i = number of shares of company i

P_i = price of stock i

β_i = beta for stock i

Weighted average beta for a portfolio consisting of two shares

A portfolio with a total value of $100 million is invested as follows: 60% in shares of company A and to 40% in shares of company B. The current share price for A is $60 whereas B is currently trading at $40 – the number of shares in both cases is therefore 1,000,000.

Assuming a beta value of 1.8 for A and 0.9 for B, the weighted average beta is calculated as follows:

$$\frac{(1{,}000{,}000 * 60 * 1.8) + (1{,}000{,}000 * 40 * 0.9)}{100{,}000{,}000} = 1.44$$

Let us assume the weighted average beta for our 50 share portfolio is 1.35. In such a case, the portfolio is expected to move 1.35 times as fast as the market (i.e. it loses 1.35% if the S&P 500 index drops by 1%) and the hedge ratio of 708 contracts is too low to cover the expected losses: the payout of the futures contract is linked to the index development and the index only drops by 1%.

To increase the accuracy of the hedge, the hedge ratio (i.e. the notional amount traded in futures contracts) has to be adjusted: if a loss of 1% in the index leads to a 1.35% loss in the portfolio, the notional amount that is sold in futures contracts should be 1.35 times higher than the portfolio value to achieve P&L neutrality.

The beta adjusted hedge ratio therefore is calculated as follows:

Equation 15

$$\text{Hedge ratio}_{\text{beta adjusted}} = \frac{\text{Current portfolio value}}{\text{Futures price} * \$250} * \text{Portfolio beta}$$

Or for our case:

$$\frac{200{,}000{,}000}{1{,}130 * 250} * 1.35 = 955.75$$

But even the adjusted hedge ratio has its shortfalls. Beta is calculated using historical price data and its value is dependent on the timeframe, i.e. the historical data used. Therefore, finding the right period for which beta should be calculated is crucial and although certain calculation concepts might have a better forecast quality than others, the future realised beta is uncertain and the ex-ante calculated adjusted hedge ratio can be proved wrong ex-post if the realised beta differs from the forecast value:

Scenario 1: equity futures down 1%, portfolio down 1.40%

The realised beta is higher than the forecasted value. The hedge ratio, i.e. the number of futures contracts sold, is too small. The portfolio was underhedged (net long stocks) and loses money.

Scenario 2: equity futures down 1%, portfolio down 1.2%

The realised beta is lower than the forecasted value. The hedge ratio, i.e. the number of futures contracts sold, was too large. The portfolio was overhedged (net short stocks) and profits from a decrease in share prices.

Scenario 3: equity futures down 1%, portfolio down 1.35%

The realised beta equals the forecasted value. The hedge ratio, i.e. the number of futures contracts sold, was correct. The portfolio was market neutral and the decrease in share prices has no P&L effect.

As we can see, the accuracy of the hedge depends on future realised beta, which can differ from the results of calculations using historical data. But although the beta adjustment does not guarantee accurate hedge ratios, such an introduction of historical price behaviour to the calculation is a state-of-the-art technique to improve hedge calculations and is used by portfolio managers all around the world.

So far, we have seen how to use index futures to set up speculative positions and how to use futures to implement hedges. Let us combine both techniques in our last example:

A US investment fund has assets of $200 million that are fully invested in S&P 500 companies. The fund does not completely replicate the index and has a beta against the S&P 500 of 1.2.

The fund manager wishes to diversify the portfolio and wants to take some temporary exposure to the Japanese market. Not being sufficiently comfortable with individual stocks in Japan, the fund manager decides to obtain exposure via the Nikkei 225 Index. The easiest way for him to do so is to take a position in the Nikkei futures traded on the CME[43], which will give the fund replication of the index without requiring any specific stock analysis. Rather than selling stocks in the portfolio, the fund manager will reduce exposure to the US market by using S&P 500 futures and plans to undertake the transaction for $40 million.

To calculate the contract number to be traded in Nikkei futures, we need to know the relevant contract specifications:

Contract size	Nikkei 225 futures price * ¥500
Expiry months	12 contracts following the March quarterly cycle (March, June, September, December). In addition to that, there are contracts for the next three serial months (serial contracts expire in months other than those in the March, June, September, and December quarterly cycle).
Quotation	Index points

[43] Futures on the Nikkei 225 are traded on the Osaka Securities Exchange, the Singapore Exchange and on the CME.

Last trading day	The last trading day is the Thursday prior to the third Friday of the expiry month, trading in the relevant contract stops at 3:15 p.m.
Settlement	Settlement of the contracts is carried out in cash to the Special Opening Quotation (SOQ) on Friday a.m. of the Nikkei 225 Index.

The current market conditions are as follows:

S&P 500 spot:	1,097
S&P 500 futures:	1,130
Nikkei 225 spot:	10,780
Nikkei 225 futures:	10,830
USD/JPY FX rate:	91.40

The first step is to calculate the partial hedge of the $ investments. As the average weighted portfolio beta is given, we can apply Equation 14:

$$\frac{40{,}000{,}000}{1{,}130 * 250} * 1.2 = 169.91$$

The fund manager therefore will sell 170 S&P 500 contracts to reduce his exposure to US markets by $40 million. To establish the position on the Japanese equity index, the fund manager will buy the Nikkei 225 futures. But how many contracts?

To answer this question, we have to transform the amount of $40 million into the equivalent ¥ (Japanese yen, JPY) amount. The USD/JPY exchange rate is given by ¥91.40 per $ so that $40 million is equal to ¥3.656 billion.

As the contract value of one Nikkei futures contract currently is ¥5,415,000, the number of futures to be bought is calculated as follows:

$$\frac{3{,}656{,}000{,}000}{10{,}830 * 500} = 675.16$$

The purchase of 675 Nikkei 225 futures will give the fund manager a risk to the Japanese stock market equivalent to a cash investment of $40 million. Using futures for such a reallocation is not only accompanied by a saving of time and transaction costs, the foreign exchange risk is minimised as well. As mentioned earlier, the futures position gives a stock market risk that is equivalent to a cash investment. The FX risk position, however, is very different.

To clarify this, let us assume that the ¥ weakens to 95 and the Nikkei (in cash index terms and futures terms) increases by 1%. The performance of a US fund will look quite different depending on whether the position has been established via futures or via cash investments:

Futures investments:

The fund manager bought the futures and the total contract value increased by 1%, which is equal to a profit of ¥36,560,000. As the fund is US based and therefore accounts in $, the profits have to be converted into ¥ using the current USD/JPY exchange rate:

$$\frac{36{,}560{,}000}{95} = \$384{,}842.11$$

Cash investments:

The fund manager sold $40 million in US stocks, sold the $ against ¥ in the spot market (initial USD/JPY cross-rate: 91.40) and invested the ¥3.565 billion in Nikkei 225 shares replicating the index. The spot index has also increased by 1% so that the performance in ¥ also equals 36,560,000. The total value of the share holdings now amounts to ¥3,692,560,000. But again: as the fund is

US based and therefore accounts in $, the amount has to be converted into $ before the profit can be calculated:

$$\frac{3{,}692{,}560{,}000.00}{95} = \$38{,}869{,}052.63$$

As the initial investment was $40 million, the cash investment results in a loss of $1,130,947.37 even though the Japanese stock market has gone up by a full percentage point. The weakening of the ¥ (by around 3.9%) has overcompensated the increase in value of the stock position denominated in ¥. In contrast to the futures investment – where only the initial margin[44] and the variation margin payments are affected by the ¥ weakening – the cash investment contains FX risk on the whole notional amount. Given the occasionally very high volatility in FX markets, this difference in risk profile means a valuable advantage of futures vs. cash in case of cross-border investments.

3.3 Interest rate futures

Interest rate futures are exchange-traded forwards with interest rates as underlying. In contrast to the equally important bond futures (which are exchange-traded forwards on government bonds with two, five, ten or 30 years' maturity), the underlying rates are interbank indicator rates (3M LIBOR, 3M EURIBOR) and interest rate futures therefore belong to the group of money market derivatives. This product feature is also reflected in the naming: the contracts that are available through NYSE Liffe are referred to as **S**hort-**T**erm **I**nterest **R**ate futures (STIR futures):

[44] We ignored the initial margin payments for simplicity. In reality, these margin payments will be affected by a ¥ weakening and lower the performance of $384,842.11. As the initial margin in comparison to the notional amount is relatively low, this effect should only be minor in comparison to the cash investment.

Underlying:	Contract name:	Contract size:
3M EURIBOR	EURIBOR futures	€1,000,000
3M £ LIBOR	Short sterling futures	£500,000
3M $ LIBOR	Eurodollar futures	$1,000,000
3M CHF LIBOR	Euroswiss futures	CHF1,000,000
3M ¥ LIBOR	Euroyen futures	¥100,000,000

As all these futures are traded on the same exchange, the contract details are very similar. To clarify the general mechanics of this type of futures, we will concentrate on the Eurodollar contracts in the following.

3.3.1 Interest rate futures mechanics

As already mentioned the STIR futures are based on money market rates as underlying. Let us have a look at the contract description for Eurodollar futures to understand how these contracts work:

Contract size	$1,000,000
Expiry months	Contracts are available for the following 20 IMM months (March, June, September, December) and for the next four serial months. That is to say there are 24 contracts in total and the first six expiry months are consecutive calendar months.
Quotation	100 minus the implied 3M interest rate.
Last trading day	Two business days prior to the third Wednesday of the expiry months. Trading stops at 11:00 London time – the time the LIBOR rates are published.

Settlement	The settlement price will be 100.000 minus the BBA[45] US$ LIBOR fixed at 11:00 London time on the last trading day rounded to multiples of 0.001.

Example

In January, a trader believes that the three months $ LIBOR fixed in mid-June will be around 1.25% and therefore higher in comparison to the current level of 1.12%. June Eurodollar futures are currently trading at 98.68. What should the trader do?

To answer that question, we first have to interpret the futures price. According to the contract definitions given above, the price of the futures is calculated as 100 minus the implied interest rate (so similar to bonds, there is an inverse price-yield relationship: implied interest rate goes up, futures price goes down). We can rearrange this simple formula and solve it for the implied interest rate. As the futures currently trade at 98.68, the implied interest rate is 1.32%. The exact description of the underlying interest rate is also given in the contract definitions: the underlying of the June contract is the 3M $ LIBOR as fixed two days prior to the third Wednesday in June. As $ LIBOR transactions have a standard settlement of T+2, the underlying is a 3M rate for investments starting on the third Wednesday of June.

The implied rate is 7 basis points higher than the expectation of our trader. To monetise his view, he has to buy futures, as a decrease in the implied rate leads to an increase in futures prices.

[45] BBA stands for British Banker Association.

It might appear a bit illogical at first sight that the trader buys futures when he expects interest rates to go up over the next few months. But this example shows why we have to compare our interest rate expectations with the market view on future interest rates and not with the current spot levels before we make investment decisions. The spot level of 3M $ LIBOR is indeed 13 basis points lower than the trader's expectation but the market has already priced in an increase in 3M $ LIBOR rates to a level of 1.32% or 20 basis points higher than the current rate. In comparison to the market view – which is expressed in the futures price – the trader expects lower rates at futures expiry. And as the final P&L of any forward transaction is driven by the difference between the agreed forward price and the settlement price (and not by the difference between initial spot rate and settlement price), the trader is right to buy futures in this case.

Let us assume the trader bought 100 contracts at a price of 98.68 and on the last trading day (third Monday of June), 3M $ LIBOR is fixed at 1.23% so that the final settlement price of the futures is 98.77. The final LIBOR is fixed 9 basis points below the market expectations at the purchase time and the trader therefore made a profit of 9 basis points. But how much is this in $?

In the previous chapter, we have introduced forward rate agreements as cash-settled forward contracts on interbank-indicator rates. For the calculation of the settlement amount, we used Equation 8:

$$DSA = \frac{\left(i_{ref} - i_{FRA}\right) * \text{Notional} * \frac{\text{Days}}{\text{Basis}}}{1 + \left(i_{ref} * \frac{\text{Days}}{\text{Basis}}\right)}$$

Applied for our futures example, the FRA rate would be given by the implied rate at trade inception and the notional would be given with $100 million (as the contract size of Eurodollar futures is $1,000,000). Assuming 92 days for the three-month period would lead to a result of:

$$DSA = \frac{(1.23\% - 1.32\%) * 100{,}000{,}000 * \frac{92}{360}}{1 + \left(1.23\% * \frac{92}{360}\right)} = -\$22{,}927.93$$

Please note that with Equation 8, we calculated the DSA from the perspective of the FRA buyer. The FRA buyer pays the FRA rate and receives the future LIBOR rate and therefore profits of a LIBOR fixing that is above the FRA rate agreed at trade inception. A long position in interest rate futures however benefits from a LIBOR fixing that is below the FRA rate agreed at trade inception so that the futures buyer has a risk position similar to the FRA seller. We can therefore conclude:

Buying FRAs is similar to selling STIR futures and vice versa.

To calculate the P&L for a long futures position we should use the DSA calculation from FRA seller's perspective. As we have learned earlier the conversion is quite simple as we just have to multiply the DSA by -1. So using the DSA formula of FRAs the P&L of the futures trader would be $22,927.93.

In practice however, we do not use this formula to calculate the P&L for interest rate futures. The formula is accurate and broadly accepted by market participants for settling FRAs, but it is not applicable for interest rate futures for the reason of contract standardisation. As we have seen in the previous chapter, the basis point value of FRAs is not constant but changes with the level of interest rates and also depends on the length of the FRA period or, to be precise, on the number of days within the forward period.

For the handling of the variation margin payments on future contracts, it would be rather impractical to have variable values per basis point and, consequently, the value per basis point is standardised by the exchange to

$25 for Eurodollar futures. The contract details set a minimum price move of 0.005 for the contracts (so half a basis point) and assign a value of $12.50 to it.[46]

The tick value of a contract can be calculated using the following formula:

$$\text{Tick value} = \text{Contract notional} * 0.005\% * \frac{90}{360}$$

For our example:

$$\begin{aligned}\text{Tick value} &= 1{,}000{,}000 * 0.005\% * \frac{90}{360} \\ &= \$12.50\end{aligned}$$

As we can see, the standardisation has two building blocks: the day count fraction of the underlying is always 0.25 (which assumes a fixed period of 90 days using a basis of 360 – even for £ contracts) and there is no discounting although the variation margin payments are made prior to the maturity of the underlying instrument. This of course is neither accurate nor in accordance to general principles of finance (namely time value of money) but these measures are necessary to make variation margins practicable.

3.3.2 Interest rate futures vs. FRAs

The differences in the design of the contracts mentioned above do not seem to be too severe at first sight. A couple of days here, a little bit of discounting there. In practice however, these minor issues lead to the need to process some very complex mathematical calculations to make both instruments comparable. This intuition behind this so-called convexity adjustment is probably best explained with another example.

[46] The minimum price change is also referred to as a tick. The tick value is the change in the P&L resulting from the futures price moving up or down by one tick ($12.50 for Eurodollar futures).

Example

DEC10 Eurodollar futures trade at 98.63 and the last trading day is the 13th December – the underlying LIBOR therefore covers a 3M period starting on the 15th December (T+2 settlement). A client wants to sell a FRA with the 3M FRA period starting on the 15th December.

? **Which price should you quote?**

It is very tempting to answer this question with 1.37% (simply the 3M rate for LIBOR investment starting on the 15/12/2010 implied by the futures contract, ignoring bid-offer spreads), as we have seen that FRAs with 3M FRA period and interest rate futures are indeed quite similar. But after having discussed some minor differences, we know that FRAs and futures contracts are similar but not identical. So should the underlying interest rate be identical?

We identified two differences caused by the need to standardise the PV01 value for futures contracts:

- The days for the underlying interest period are standardised to 90
- The variation margin and final settlement payments are made without discounting

As the FRA period (15/12/2010-15/03/2010) also contains 90 days, we can ignore the first bullet point for our case. The second bullet point however deserves closer attention.

Earlier, we mentioned that selling a FRA is similar to buying futures contracts. Let us therefore compare a long futures position with the position of a FRA seller for different scenarios:

	Long futures	FRA sold
Notional/number of contracts	100 futures ($100,000,000)	$100,000,000
Expiry/settlement date:	15/12/2010	15/12/2010
Underlying days:	90	90
Initial price/FRA rate:	98.63%	1.37%
P&L for relevant LIBOR fixing at 1.37%	0.00	0.00
P&L for relevant LIBOR fixing at 1.07%	$75,000	$74,799.91
P&L for relevant LIBOR fixing at 1.67%	–$75,000	–$74,688.18

At first sight, none of the two alternatives seems to be advantageous: the FRA seller gains less in case of a decrease in rates but also loses less in case of a rate increase in comparison to the futures buyer.

But let us calculate the notional that the FRA seller should trade to gain $75,000 in case of the rate decreasing to 1.07% and use the adjusted notional to recalculate the scenarios:

$$\text{Adjusted notional}_{FRA} = 100{,}000{,}000 * \frac{75{,}000}{74{,}799.91} = 100{,}267{,}500$$

	Long futures	FRA sold
Notional/number of contracts	100 futures ($100,000,000)	$100,267,500
P&L for relevant LIBOR fixing at 1.07%	$75,000	$75,000
P&L for relevant LIBOR fixing at 1.67%	–$75,000	–$74,887.97

Now it is obvious that the selling of a FRA should be preferred to a long position in futures: in case of a decrease in rates, both positions will have an identical profit but in case of a rate increase, the FRA seller will lose less than the futures buyer. Extending the range of scenarios will make the advantage of FRAs vs. futures even more obvious:

	Long futures	FRA sold
P&L for relevant LIBOR fixing at 0.87%	$125,000	$125,062.36
P&L for relevant LIBOR fixing at 1.87%	–$125,000	–$124,751.16

But how can this phenomenon be explained? In Section 2.2.4, we discussed the convexity profile of FRAs and concluded that due to the calculation of the DSA, the seller of a FRA is long convexity: the increase of profits accelerates the further interest rates are falling and the increase in losses decelerates the further interest rates are rising.

The payoff function for interest rate futures however is linear as their PV01 is fixed by the exchange ($25 per basis point in case of Eurodollar futures) and is independent from the current level of interest rates. This difference in convexity profiles (also referred to as discounting bias) leads to the fact that in case of implied futures rates equalling the FRA rate and the fixing rate being different from the rate agreed at trade inception, the FRA sold position will always outperform the long futures position.

In addition to the mentioned discounting bias, the margin system for futures is the reason for another and – especially for long-dated contracts – more weighty advantage of a FRA sold position in comparison to a long futures position: the holder of a long futures position will receive margin payments if yields fall and will have to pay variation margin in case of a rate increase. At first sight, this seems to be a symmetric risk profile but if we assume a reasonably high positive correlation between futures prices and spot interest rates, we will see that the profile is not at all symmetric: the futures buyer receives variation margin payments when rates have fallen and can only invest the money at lower rates. In case of a rise in rates however, the futures buyer has to pay the variation margin and has to fund these payments at higher rates.

Both advantages lead to the fact that we will hardly ever find implied futures rates and the relevant FRA rates trading at exactly the same level in practice. As the FRA position is clearly more attractive in comparison to the futures, futures prices will trade slightly lower than calculated by using the relevant FRA rate and subtracting it from 100 – the futures buyer should receive compensation to go long the short-term rates using futures and giving up the described advantages of FRAs. Vice versa, the FRA rate will be slightly lower than the implied futures rate. In other words: the seller of a FRA will profit "later" in case of a rate decrease in comparison to the futures buyer, as his benchmark rate (the FRA rate) is lower than the benchmark rate for the futures buyer – this way the FRA seller implicitly "pays" compensation for being long the advantageous instrument.

The difference between implied futures rates and the relevant FRA rate is also referred to as convexity adjustment and can be calculated using relatively complex mathematical methods that are not discussed in detail in this book but as being long convexity only gives advantage in case of a move in interest rates, it is obvious that one of the main influencing factors of the convexity adjustment is the expected future volatility of the underlying interest rate.

Exercise

1. You are working as an equity portfolio manager and are looking to hedge 50% of your $100 million portfolio to reduce your exposure prior to the earning season that you expect to show mixed results. If the beta of your portfolio is 0.9 to the S&P 500 index, how many futures do you have to trade and do you have to buy or sell the contracts? Please assume the S&P currently trades at a level of 1,052.

2. You are trading short-term interest rates for a major US based investment bank. The implied rate in March 2011 short sterling contracts is 1.65% and you believe that the actual fixing will be much higher.

   a) Assuming you sold 250 contracts at 98.35 and the final £ LIBOR fixing takes place at 2.13%, please calculate your P&L in £.

   b) Further assuming an initial margin of £650 per contract and a strengthening of USD against GBP from 1.65 to 1.52, please calculate the relevant P&L on a USD basis.

Research Tasks

1. Please have a look at your derivatives pricing system and talk to your colleagues from the trading desk to answer the following questions:
   - What are the current convexity adjustments for the Eurodollar strip?
   - How can we find the market expectation for future volatility of the underlying rates?
   - Which factors (other than volatility) are mainly influencing the convexity adjustment?

Solutions

Chapter 2

1. a) $12 * \left[1 + (3.20\% - 1.70\%) * \frac{92}{360}\right] = 12.046$

   b) The dividend payment date no longer falls into the forward period. The adjusted dividend yield for the forward period will now be zero – even if the actual amount is expected to be higher. A decrease in dividend yields leads to the cost of carry to increase which – all other things being equal – leads to an increase of the forward price. As you sold the shares forward at a lower price, the P&L effect would be negative.

   c) New forward: $12.34 * \left[1 + (3.15\%) * \frac{91}{360}\right] = 12.438$

   Mark to market: $\frac{(12.046 - 12.438)}{\left(1 + 3.15\% * \frac{91}{360}\right)} * 100{,}000 = 38{,}915.86$

2. a) The buyer of a FRA pays the FRA rate and receives the floating rate – he therefore generally benefits from an increase in rates. However, as an increase in rates also leads to a higher discounting effect, every basis point increase is worth less than the previous one: the FRA buyer is short convexity.

   The FRA bought is a 4*11 FRA which means the underlying rate is a seven-month rate with the investment period starting in four months' time. Consequently, the PV01 vector should show values in the four-month and in the 11-month bucket.

   We can calculate the PV01 vector by shifting the four-month rate up by 1 basis point, recalculating the forward and do a mark-to-market valuation using the new implied forward rate. The same process will then be repeated for the 11-month rate.

Initial FRA rate: $\left(\frac{\left(1+2.80\% * \frac{334}{365}\right)}{\left(1+3.20\% * \frac{120}{365}\right)} - 1\right) * \frac{365}{(334-120)} = 2.5489\%$

4M: new forward rate after shifting the 4M rate up by 1bp: 2.5433%

Mark-to-market valuation:

$$\frac{(2.5433\% - 2.5489\%) * 250{,}000{,}000 * \frac{(334-120)}{365}}{\left(1+2.80\% * \frac{334}{365}\right)} = -8{,}048.67$$

11M: new forward rate after shifting the 11M rate up by 1bp: 2.5643%

Mark-to-market valuation:

$$\frac{(2.5643\% - 2.5489\%) * 250{,}000{,}000 * \frac{(334-120)}{365}}{\left(1+2.81\% * \frac{334}{365}\right)} = 22{,}071.02$$

b) As interest rates have gone up in comparison to the agreed FRA rate, the FRA buyer will receive the payment:

$$\frac{(3\% - 2.5489\%) * 250{,}000{,}000 * \frac{(214)}{365}}{\left(1+3\% * \frac{214}{365}\right)} = 649{,}793.72$$

3. a) The interest rate of the primary currency is marginally lower than the interest rate of the primary currency. The FX forward therefore should be higher than the spot, i.e. GBP weakens vs. euro on a forward basis.

b) The FX forward can be calculated as follows:

$$FX_{spot} * \frac{1 + 1.89\% * \frac{182}{365}}{1 + 1.85\% * \frac{182}{360}} = 0.87006$$

c) In case of identical interest rates in the primary and in the secondary currency, we would normally expect the forward FX rate to equal the spot FX rate. As the day count convention in EUR is ACT/360 whereas in GBP money markets we use ACT/365, the forward FX in this case differs from the spot FX:

$$FX_{spot} * \frac{1 + 1.85\% * \frac{182}{365}}{1 + 1.85\% * \frac{182}{360}} = 0.86989$$

We can conclude that the forward FX rate will only equal the spot FX rate if the day count adjusted interest rates of primary and secondary currency are identical.

d)

£ depreciation	6M £ rate increase	6M € rate increase
Positive MTM	Positive MTM	Negative MTM

Chapter 3

1. To hedge a long position in shares, you have to sell futures. The beta adjusted hedge ratio for this case is calculated as follows:

$$\frac{50{,}000{,}000}{1{,}052 * 250} * 0.9 = 171.10266$$

To hedge 50% of your portfolio, you have to sell 171 S&P 500 futures contracts. Please note: as beta is below 1, the beta adjustment in this case leads to a lower number of contracts than in case of a non-beta-adjusted hedge (ignoring beta, the hedge ratio would be 190 futures contracts).

2. a) To calculate the P&L in sterling, you simply have to calculate the number of basis points the market moved in your favour and multiply this value with the PV01 of the underlying contract and the number of contracts traded. Please note: as the contract value of sterling futures is 500,000, their PV01 value is £12.50. Consequently, the P&L is calculated as follows:

$$[98.35 - (100 - 2.13)] * 100 * 12.50 * 250 = £150{,}000$$

b) The total P&L on a USD basis has to take the currency depreciation (GBP weakened in comparison to USD) into account. A weakening in GBP is disadvantageous for two reasons:

1. The variation margin received in USD terms is now worth less than it would have been before: using the old exchange rate of 1.65, the £150,000 payment would have had a $ value of 247,500 – as GBP has depreciated, the £150,000 payment is only worth $228,000.

2. The initial margin that will be received back after closing out the position has a lower $ value than at trade inception. To buy the required GBP $(250 * £650 = £162{,}500)$, you initially paid $268,125. Selling the amount after receiving it back from the

exchange (and here, we assume for simplicity that there are no interest rate payments for the initial margin) will only give you \$247,000 so that there is a currency related loss of \$21,125 from the initial margin transaction.

In USD, the total P&L effect therefore is:

$$\$228{,}000 - \$21{,}125 = \$206{,}875.$$

Please note: we have ignored funding costs (to buy the £162,500 needed as initial margin, we need to borrow \$268,125) and any interest rate payment on the initial margin account for simplicity. In reality however, the total P&L calculation would have to be adjusted by funding costs and interest income that accrue during the term of the trade.